Immersion into the Shadows
Effective Method Of Dark Psychology

Immersion into the Shadows
Effective Method Of Dark Psychology

How To Use The Best Persuasion Techniques To Achieve Your Best Goals And How To Protect Yourself From Being Manipulated

King Black

A & P Publishing LLC

Immersion into the Shadows
Effective Method Of Dark Psychology
How To Use The Best Persuasion Techniques To
Achieve Your Best Goals And How To Protect Yourself
From Being Manipulated
be King Black

Introduction

The dark side of our society is everywhere. Whether or not we are aware that it exists, it has an impact on our lives, our dreams and our ability to achieve.

People who have been able to master the techniques of dark psychology, and discover the hidden techniques of manipulation have experienced tremendous results throughout their lives. Not only have they used the techniques of dark psychology to remove the obstacles that prevent them from achieving success, but they have used the same techniques to prevent those who commit dark psychology manipulation techniques from achieving their goals.

This book is a practical guide that will enable you to understand how dark psychology affects our behavior. It will also teach you the most effective methods of manipulation, as well as persuasion techniques to ensure that you will have a mindset that allows you to experience the most that life has to offer.

The book begins by explaining to you the concept of dark psychology, as well as the main factors that drive it. The aim of this book is to make you understand the fact that dark psychology is part of all human beings, with the caveat that some people use it more often than others.

The book also provides information on the different types of dark personality in psychology and their characteristics. In this way, you will be able to recognize when you are being surrounded by the specific type of Dark personality and protect yourself from becoming its victim.

There are many methods and tools used to manipulate

people in secret. Each personality type makes use of one tool or technique over another. It all depends on the purpose. The book provides important information about these techniques and tools used by manipulators to control and dominate their victims. The purpose of this book is to help you avoid becoming their victim and, more importantly, to protect your family members from falling into their traps. If there are people who have already fallen into the trap, this book offers suggestions on how to help them escape and free themselves.

Chapter 1: The Nature of Dark Psychology

All people have a dark side. For example, almost all of us have been deceived in one way or another to avoid consequences (or punishment) or for some benefit or gain, or some other reason.

In a sense, those who consider themselves "street wise" or "street smart" are adept at using "any means necessary" to achieve their goals. Behind "any means necessary" are a myriad of "dirty tricks," such as deception and brainwashing, indoctrination, seduction, hypnotization, emotional or psychological manipulation, and many others. These "dirty tricks" exist in the shadows so that people do not see the "tricks" when they are being employed. The lucky person later discovers that he or she has been a victim of "dirty tricks".

Some of these dirty tricks are accepted by the public and are considered part of "lite psychology". For example, rewards or prizes, praise and free tokens are considered a motivational incentive, but are somehow used to manipulate the mind (in politics, business diplomacy, religious leadership) and sexual seduction (in romance). They are believed to be part of white psychology (or "light psychology"). Therefore, they are not considered dirty because they have been cleansed by good intentions.

The dark "light" and the light

The most important distinction between "dark tricks" (or dirty tricks) and "light tricks" (or white tricks) lies in purpose.

The main purpose of using "dark tricks" is to selfishly benefit from others no matter what they lose.

However, the purpose of using "white tricks" is to create more good for other people. This can be, in a sense, an exchange of benefits.

For example, gifts can be employed as a dirty trick or as a black trick. If the intent of the gift is to lure an individual into the hands of a serial killer, then it is a dirty trick. However, if the intent of the gift is to motivate the child to be more successful in school, it is an unintentional trick.

Similarly, the distinction between white and dark psychology lies in intentions.

What is meant by dark psychology?

The term "dark psychology" refers to the wild human traits that are inherent in every human being. The degree of predisposition to this dark psychological trait varies from one individual to another.

Some people are less prone to dark psychology than others. For some the predisposition is minimal, while for others it is moderate. For the minority who are very active. They are the ones who tend to be more prone to use dark psychology. It is part of the dark trifecta (psychopathic narcissists, psychopaths, as well as Machiavellians).

2. What is dark about this psychology?

Different people have their own definition of what "dark" means in the field of dark psychology. Some have even tried to define "dark" psychology.

Without setting aside established definitions, it is essential to know the context of the definition that is relevant to this book. The best method for determining the definition is to use an explanation of the context that after the conclusion of the chapter, you come up with your personal conclusion.

The book explores dark psychology within the perspective that of our subconscious minds (and the unconscious mind). This is known as a "dark mind - one that is unaware of reality.

In this sense and with respect to the idea of survival of the fittest which is a proof of the existence of the primitive animal instinct we all possess to fight against obstacles, we see dark psychology as the study, exploration, refinement and use of sources accessed by the distinctive characteristics that the unconscious mind has, which help to ensure the survival of human beings. We might loosely refer to these features as blind spots. Indeed, but the Dark Triad personalities are different in the sense that they do not rely on Dark psychology to fulfill the survival instinct, but rather because of their twisted need to harm others.

But as the words are not just the semantic term "blind spot" is not just a fancy word. It also means the state of mind, the intention, as well as the possibility of.

3 blind spots in dark psychology

As we have said blind spots are atypical features that are associated with the unconscious mind. Like the blind spots we know with respect to sight blind spots are also isolated units that are not accessible to the light of consciousness. However, the fact that their existence is recognized makes it possible to use, explore and exploit them for the benefit of the process that takes place in the light of consciousness.

Some of the most well-known problems of dark psychology are.

* Genetic influences
* Self-identity
* Instinct
* Self-interest

4 Genetic (and epigenetic) influences

It has been scientifically proven that genetics transmits information regarding certain genetic abnormalities such as addiction to promiscuity, addiction, etc. This means that there are people who are genetically predisposed to be addicts, promiscuous or murderers, etc.

Similarly, genetics is an important factor in dark psychology, as it transmits the traits of twisted ancestors to their offspring, thus facilitating the development of similar traits to their children.

5- Self-identity

The search for self-identity begins at an early age. It is strongly influenced by genes and affected by the environment.

These are the essential components of your identity as a person:

* Your identity
* Your ego
* Your super ego
* Your energy cathexis

6- Your ID

The Id is the most basic aspect of self-identity. It is the place where the animal instinct to seek pure pleasure is fixed, regardless of the consequences. It is here that the pleasure principle reigns.

Moreover, it is in this area of the Id where the rule is to avoid pain at all costs. In the Id it does not matter whether the pain is directed at altruistic motives or whether it produces greater benefits in the end. Pain, in any form, will not be tolerated.

Id is the reason for the pleasure principle, which is the most important principle and superior to all other principles.

Id is devoid of all reality. The Id is the result of fundamental processes that satisfy its desires. These fundamental processes, as outlined by Dr. Freud (a reputed psychologist), consist of satisfying basic survival needs, such as self-protection, thirst, hunger and other needs, which are usually expressed by infants.

Libido is the main source of energy that drives the Id. Libido is often associated with sexual desire. But libido is much more than sexual desire. It is about the forms of energy that create arousal to satisfy basic desires through fundamental processes.

There are two main instincts that are responsible for driving Id. They are:

Eros

Thanatos

Eros is the basic instinct that drives motivation to the pleasure-seeking process of the primal.

Thanatos, however, is the primal instinct that drives

motivation toward the destruction of self and others. In fact, it is Thanatos that is the reason for the drive to murder or destroy property, commit suicide and other things.

7- Your ego

The ego is the world-conscious component of self-identity. In contrast to the Id the ego is not in a state of numbness to reality.

While the Id operates within the pleasure principle, the ego functions through the reality principle.

The ego is able to communicate with reality, and discern what is real as well as the results of certain behaviors caused by basic processes.

The ego is the only way we are able to understand the meaning of social norms in the larger perspective of the self.

The ego uses other methods such as recognition perception and perception judgment and memory to figure out how to interact with others in a more effective and mutually beneficial way.

The ego is formed throughout childhood and reaches its peak by the age of. But it develops in a limited way in the years after childhood and throughout the rest of adult life.

8- Ego vs Id

In the realm of self-identity, there is always a struggle with the Ego Id and the Id. Sometimes, the ego wins but other times the Id wins.

The ego seeks to balance the Id and manipulate it so that it is in tune with reality rather than acting as a primitive, blind instinct that is not part of any realization.

It could be said that the Ego can be described as the great eye of the Id. It helps the Id navigate the world and use its enormous energy for the pursuit of the greater purpose of the self.

9- Your Super Ego

While the Id is based on the joy principle and the ego on the reality principle, the Superego is based on the consciousness principle.

The principle of conscience is primarily concerned with moral laws and tries to adhere to the morals of the society, the values of the organization, as well as the cultural ethos and other similar principles.

The main objective is to discern what is right and what is wrong, and to strive to eliminate the wrong while advocating for the right.

The desire for justice in the rule of law, fairness, and equity are aspects of the superego.

The superego depends on the ideal model of the ego which it uses as a model to determine the direction and performance of its ego.

The superego is an antidote to the primitive desires of the Id, such as the desire for sexual pleasure and aggression.

10- Id vs Ego vs Superego

The ego is always in struggle to keep the desires of the Id and Superego within the confines of reality.

The Id is responsible for managing higher level mental processes such as problem solving, reasoning and logic.

The ego makes use of these higher levels of mental faculties to resolve the Id-Superego issue, devising ways to keep the fundamental desires of the Id within the constraints of the Superego.

We know, for example, the importance of sexual intimacy and the importance of combating hunger and thirst. These needs must be satisfied for the human being to be healthy, fully functioning and balanced. But, if the ego does not control the Id, the person could resort to rape to satisfy sexual desire. One could also decide to rob food stores to satiate the desire to eat, and also to satiate the desire to drink water. The ego will introduce the fact that when it comes to sexual relations there should be agreement and negotiation, not the use of force. It will also bring to light the fact that, in order to combat thirst and hunger, one must work hard to earn money to buy food and water. In addition, one must use a higher degree of thinking to borrow or beg for these items.

War is not good because of super interest. Also, war is not necessary. What happens when you are innocently attacked by an attacker who depends on a primitive Id and whose ego is so overwhelming to the Id? If the Superego is dominant in this scenario and is not able to counteract the ego, then the victim has to not engage in self-defense in order to stay out of the war, and thus suffer punishments of being taken away or enslaved. They can also be or even killed. It is clear that the reality is quite different. The ego is likely to assert that "yes, it is true that war is bad, but it is even more harmful not to protect oneself and one's family, children and loved ones from destructive forces." In this sense, the ego is likely to use this truth - reason and reasoning - to fight to defend itself. Of course, when it comes to self-defense the ego will defend itself against the Id by using excessive force or destructive acts to defend itself.

These three forces are significant. However, they are strong. As we all know, absolute power is the most destructive thing that can happen. Responsibility without power is a risk. Likewise, powerlessness that is not accompanied by responsibility can be equally risky. Hence the requirement to have the Id or Superego to be balanced with the Ego's tools of reasoning, problem solving and logic.

11. Your energetic cathexis

Cathexis is the process of investing energy in various service enterprises. According to Freud, the potencies resulting from the Id (primitive impulses), the Ego and the Super Ego are all forms of energy.

Thus, the energy of sensory stimulation is transformed into psychic energy when it comes into contact and encounter with stimuli.

Freud states that psychic energy is processed through various associative language metaphors embedded in the topographical model of the person. The filtered energy is released through the unconscious subconscious (subconscious) and finally through the conscious mind.

It is easy to believe that what we see through our senses is instantly consumed and processed by our conscious mind. However, according to Freud, this is not the reality. Perceptions are processed by the unconscious mind, and are transferred to the subconscious mind, and then transformed into reality by consciousness.

Understanding this process is crucial. It allows us to

understand the crucial role played by the subconscious and the conscious (preconscious) mind. To understand a person's identity and the motivations behind a person's behavior, it is crucial to examine the role played by the subconscious and the unconscious mind. It is also essential to consider the topographical model that is responsible for filtering and converting this energy into real.

Back to cathexis. To better understand and appreciate the various roles played by the cathexis we must understand its underlying nature.

Cathexis is divided into three main components:

* Object cathexis - Refers to the Id's effort to invest energy in the object image. It also refers to the energy expended in interacting with an object. For example, if a person is hungry, he invests his energy in the image of the preferred food, such as Pizza or a pizza; and if he is in search of the supernatural solution the person invests his energy in gods.

* Ego-catexis - Refers to the Ego's involvement in the mental representation of reality through the use of language (associations or metaphors) as a precondition to the other Ego processes. For example, that desire to eat a cake at lunchtime is hindered by the reality of "keeping score," meaning that it requires going to the cafeteria at lunchtime.

* Anti-catexis is the energy expended or invested through the Ego and Super-ego to impede object-catexis. In this way, anti-catexis functions as a brake on the primary desires of the Id. For example, the desire to eat a piece of cake at lunchtime is blocked by having to fast during the day to help the less fortunate.

12 The role of self-identity Dark psychology.

Based on this understanding of self-identity, we discern that a person's identity is greatly affected by influences beyond the influence of the environment. It is innate and shaped by genetics.

For example, if one has a weak anticatexis with respect to eros, one is likely to be sexually promiscuous, sexually intoxicated, or even a serial sexual predator. However, when one has an unreliable anti-catexis regarding Thanatos and Thanatos, then the person will more likely be a murderer, sadist or even the victim of serial murder.

In Dark psychology where the Id reigns supreme, free of ego boundaries or anti-catexis is where the Dark Continuum is found. The center in this Dark Continuum where the malevolent gravitational pull is the strongest, can be found is that the Dark Singularity exists.

The Dark Continuum

The Dark Continuum refers to an imaginary conceptual space (often represented in concentric circles) in which malevolent behavior can be found. These malevolent actions could be Machiavellianism narcissism and psychopathy. Signs of this may include violent, sadistic, criminal, etc. behavior.

Dark Continuity Dark Continuity is often figuratively connected to the dark point of the galaxy or the sun. In our case, it is possible to relate the Dark Continuum to the "blind spot" discussed above.

In the Dark Continuum reside perceptions, thoughts, feelings, as well as experiences (from previous actions of humans).

In dark psychology, the Dark Continuum is used as a

conceptual measure to gauge the extreme or severity in the range of terrible to even more. The scale ranges from moderate and purposeful to extreme and purposeless.

It is in the area of mild and purposeful that Dark Psychology can be converted to positive effects. It is in this area that subtle and covert uses of dark psychology can be used to benefit the person who is applying it.

In the realm of the harsh and unintended (which is the exact opposite that is gentle and purposeful) there is more overt and violent destruction. Violent destruction not only has the potential to cause harm to the victims, but also to the perpetrator. It is in this region that the thoughts possessed by serial killers, violent sexual rapists, and people who self-harm (e.g., suicide bombers, addicts, those who self-immolate, as well as those who commit suicide in the normal way, etc.) are found.

The dark singularity
The dark singularity can be described as the final central point of the Dark Continuum. It is similar to the central point of a galaxy's black hole.

Another way to look at it is to think of lunar eclipses as an analogy. In this case, the Dark Singularity is the umbra, and the Dark Continuum is the "penumbra". In this sense, Dark psychology refers to the dark shadow that exists in both the penumbra and the umbra.

In the field of psychology the Dark Singularity is considered the most evil point of Dark psychology. This is where pure evil takes its pure form. In it lies the pure power of destruction that is not ignited by any reasonable, moral or deliberate motive. This is the place exactly where the Dark cathexis can be at its best.

In this Dark Singularity rests the intense desire to destroy, for no reason whatsoever. In this moment, there are the most primitive animal desires that are the hallmark of psychopaths, narcissists and sadists. In this realm where serial killers, vampires and cannibals are part of the picture.

Dark psychology as an inherent aspect of survival of the fittest.

Nothing explains the concept of survival of the fittest better than Darwin's Theory of Evolution, in which the fittest are able to pass on their genes to succeeding generations.

In the process of ovulation, there are millions of sperm fighting for the egg. Only one sperm is able to fertilize the egg and, consequently, create the birth of a new creature. The millions that fail die in a battle for the strongest.

If you look at yourself, you will realize that you are a descendant of the fittest... in the world of ovulation.

What are you surviving against?

In the epic novel called "the animal farm" there is a constant struggle for survival. Even when there is the concept of equality, some animals fare better than others.

Our genes are designed for the survival of the fittest. Genetic information regarding changes over time, current environmental conditions and risks for the future, as well as the potential for future risks are passed on to the next generation, allowing the next generation to have a better chance of being able to survive.

Different genes are not created equal. Well-crafted genes

produce healthy creatures that are capable of surviving in the environment they are expected to inhabit and poorly crafted genes are a swarm of deadly explosions (genetic anomalies.... (or a "genetic evil") whose beings are wiped out by genetic diseases. Sickle cell anemia is an exemplary illustration of this genetic disease.

Although genetic transformation can take time, epigenesis appears to be a faster reaction that attaches epigenetic data to the surface of genes, without significantly altering the structure of the DNA, nor its information. The epigenetic code is intended to aid in the survival of the next offspring (e.g., an embryo in the womb) or for the immediate next generation.

Another intriguing concept is neuroplasticity, which explains how the brain is able to adapt to its environment by changing the activities of our organism that no longer serve and intensifying those that do.

Our immune system works in the same way: by being friends with microorganisms that kill foreign microorganisms that are at their point of entry.

In the battle for the strongest, you will observe that our consciousness is only a small portion of the iceberg, the vast iceberg underneath is the dark realm - one that is part of your subconscious. As much as we have tried to understand the intricacies of this dark endeavor, there are still many mysteries to be solved.

However, those who decided to dive down to investigate the depths and shape of this massive Iceberg have discovered the nuggets of dark and mysterious secrets that lie beneath the subterranean sphere. They have uncovered some of these secrets and have learned how to use them to gain advantage and conquer their respective zones of influence.

The purpose of this publication is to open the secrets of this book to your awareness. The primary objective is to help you protect yourself from those with hidden weapons that can prevent the dark and dangerous world that could harm you. The second objective is to help you use these dark secrets to become one of the strongest survivors in this extremely aggressive and violently competitive and destructive world.

Chapter 2: Dark Psychology Personality Types

In the field of psychology, a person's type is a set of characteristics and traits that make a person more prone to an inherited set of behavioral characteristics.

In the same way, dark psychology has its distinct personality types. There are three main personality types that are identified within dark psychology.

These three personality types are

Narcissism (entitled self-importance)

Machiavellianism (strategic exploitation and deception)

Psychopathy (callousness and cynicism).

The dark triad

The three personality types mentioned above are found in Dark psychology, although distinct, they are closely interrelated and interdependent to the point of having certain fundamental characteristics.

The close interrelationship and interdependence between the three distinct personality types is known as "the Dark Triad".

Thus, "the Dark Triad" is a psychological term used to

describe the interrelationship between the three basic personality types that make up dark psychology. They are like a three-legged stool on which dark psychology rests as a foundation.

A crucial point to remember is that the Dark Triad only encompasses the nonclinical elements. For example, it consists of nonclinical (or nonpathological) psychopathy and narcissism.

Pathological or clinical narcissism and psychopathy are mental disorders that require psychiatric or psychotherapeutic intervention.

Machiavellianism is not a condition with pathological or clinical aspects. Narcissism that is not pathological or clinical and psychopathy, although not the norm, are considered normal in any particular population.

In this book we will concentrate on the nonpathological or nonclinical components that make up dark psychology. We will leave the clinical and pathological cases to the guidance of the psychiatric literature.

The dark factor (D-factor)

There are fundamental characteristics that can be shared among the three Dark Triad personality types.

These fundamental attributes are called The Dark Factor. This Dark Factor is the key factor that drives this Dark Psychology.

In essence, the Dark aspect refers to the dark and evil aspects of human nature, which are characterized by the following 9 main characteristics:

Selfishness

Self-interest
Psychological entitlement
Moral detachment
Spitefulness
Sadism
Machiavellianism
Narcissism
Psychopathy

1. Selfishness

Selfishness is defined as a focus on one's own personal gains, without regard for the costs, losses or harm inflicted on other people. As we have discussed the aspect of self-identity and egoism, the cathexis of the anti-ego is so weak that the super-ego does not have it and the Id dominates.

2- Self-interest

Self-interest is defined by a strong drive to achieve and display the individual's social and financial position.

3. Psychological entitlement

Psychological entitlement is a recurrent perception of one-self as superior to others, and therefore deserving of superior treatment.

4- Moral disengagement

Moral disengagement refers to a mental processing technique that allows individuals to indulge in illegal behavior, without any feelings of discomfort (such as guilt, or regret).

5- Spitefulness

Spitefulness is the naive desire to cause harm to others, regardless of the risk of being hurt in the process.

6-Sadism

Sadism is a way of obtaining pleasure through the act of causing harm to other people, whether for personal advantage or not.

7- Machiavellianism

Machiavellianism is a very cunning and manipulative mentality based on the notion that the goal is greater than the method.

8- Narcissism

Narcissism is the tendency to excessive self-absorption, which results in a heightened illusion of superiority and an insatiable desire for attention from other people.

9- Psychopathy

Psychopathy is the total absence of empathy that is accompanied by an incapacity for self-control that results in aggressive behavior.

Machiavellian personality type

The Machiavellian personality type is the most prevalent. It is a learned personality type. It is considered normal within society. For example, most politicians are Machiavellian in nature. Similarly, many religious figures are Machiavellian in nature. It is, therefore, an extremely popular character type, despite its obscure origins.

Machiavellianism is also the only personality type within the dark trio that does not suffer from any pathological extremes.

The following are the most important characteristics of this personality type: Machiavellian person:

* Very deceitful

* Lack of respect for others

Use of other people to achieve their own personal goals * No concern for others

* No concern for others

* Extremely manipulative

* Very uncooperative

* Low moral ethics

* Obsessive

* Extremely resourceful

* Risk-taker in the pursuit of new opportunities

* Pleasure-seeking

They are high risk takers, but are extremely intelligent, prudent and cautious in securing their gains.

* Although they are extremely impulsive in making quick decisions, they are able to make objective decisions (free of emotional impulses) for long-term strategy.

* Fear of merger (i.e., an emotional fear of being connected to other people)

Narcissistic personality type

The narcissistic personality type is the second most dominant of the three Dark Triad personality types.

The following are the most important characteristics of the narcissistic type:

*Self-imputation is a way of establishing superiority.

* Epiphanic perspective

* Infallibility

* Assumption of the desire of others to know more and experience.

*Monopolic tendency to possess and separate those around them from the rest of the population.

* False modesty

* Only gives the origin of its narcissistic source.

* The use of projection to defend themselves from psychological attacks.

* They present the dissociative gap, as well as confabulation.

* Believe they are above the law

* Disruptive

* Resent authority

* Counter-dependent

* Pretend to be immune to what happens to them if they do.

* Show self-centered rage

* They are unfriendly to disagreement and criticism.

The types of narcissists who are:

* Overt (straight) narcissists

* Covert (inverted) narcissists

* Malignant narcissists

Different types of narcissism

* Pathological narcissism

* Healthy (therapeutic) narcissism

Psychopathic personality type

The psychopathic personality type is the least known among the 3 personality types of the dark trinity. However, it is the most dangerous of them all. Its power can be very dangerous when combined with narcissism or Machiavellianism.

Joseph Stalin is probably the best known example that best embodies the ideal combination of the three personality types that make up the Dark Triad, through which they came together to form a grandiose and dangerous character.

Here are some of the most prominent traits of the psychopathic personality type:

* Great risk takers

* Fearless

* Very deceptive

* Extreme lack of empathy

* Cold-hearted

* Calm

* Very arrogant

* Very superficial charm

* Absence of remorse

* Manipulative masters

Poor judgment, do not learn from past consequences

Egocentric and in a position to create long term relationships * Glibness

* Glibness

* Self-esteem and self-importance.

Chapter 3 The methodology of dark psychology and its applications

Many psychological techniques have two purposes: they can be used for white and dark psychology. What is different is the intention of the person using the methods.

In this chapter we will discuss psychological methods used to achieve nefarious ends.

Dark Persuasion

Persuasion is the most popular psychological technique. It is most often employed to aid white psychology. It is a tool used for White psychology, most of us have used it in one way or another. However, only a few have used persuasion to use it as a dark psychology tool.

Before we delve into the depths of Dark persuasion, let's look at the essential elements of persuasion in everyone.

1. **What is persuasion?**

Persuasion refers to the psychological method of presenting arguments as to motivate to change, influence or alter the attitudes or behavior of an individual, in order to achieve the desired result.

2- **Tips for persuasion**

These are the most important guidelines you should learn in order to succeed in your persuasive skills:

Do your homework to find reliable and authoritative information.

- Be a thought leader to guide others in their thinking.

* Have faith in yourself

* Appeal to feelings

* Make use of rhetorical phrases and statements.

* Limit sarcasm to a minimum

* Sound reasonable

* Watch for reactions

* Be discreet in the way you respond

* Listen carefully

* Suggest, don't demand

* Be attentive

* Be emotionally intelligent

3- Persuasion tactics

The following are fundamental but crucial persuasion strategies:

* Introduce the names of the people you are interacting with.

* Create an intimate connection

* Creating relationships

* Offering the possibility of reciprocity

* Use motivational words

* Be agile and dynamic Like a chameleon alter your approach to suit the specificity of your target (no broad approach). Use the NLP method of mirroring, matching or matching.

* Benefit from the Bandwagon effect.

* Instill a fear image in the minds of those you are convincing.

* Stimulate curiosity by creating a vacuum of information (suspense)

* Apply the "foot in the front door" tactic: make a small request so that the door will open and allow a larger request.

Be clear about the advantages of your idea for the person you are trying to convince. Be aware that every person is prone to ask "what good is this to me?".

The Bandwagon Effect

The Bandwagon effect is the influence that a group of people exerts on its members.

The following are some typical characteristics associated with the bandwagon phenomenon.

"Herd mentality" people are attracted to follow others.

* Social proof - People tend to adhere to the most popular cause of action. For example, denouncing a negative social proof (such as littering, cutting down trees, excessive smoking, etc.) can actually increase the likelihood of its occurrence. For example, in the case of absenteeism at 20, instead of pointing out the increase in absenteeism from the previous 15% to 20%, the manager should emphasize the positive social proof of the situation by calling out the vast majority of employees who are not absent (i.e., 80%) and referring to the 20% as a few virgin apples to be relegated to the back of the closet.

Fraud

To deceive means to deliberately and willfully propagate something that is not authentic with the intent to obscure, mislead, or propagate a particular idea, belief, or notion in order to influence the target to do something or behave in a specific way.

Deception, in other words, is the manipulation of appearances to suggest the illusion of truth.

The main objective of deception is to conceal. The most common deception techniques are:

* Propaganda - spreading false information and presenting it as fact or truth.

* Camouflage - hiding the real essence of things. For example, a spy using philanthropy to penetrate the community.

* Pretense - taking the form of a lie that differs from the real form. For example, pretending to be innocent when one

is guilty, pretending to be sick, or pretending to be sorry while celebrating a party, etc.

* Mitigation: creating a sense of supernaturalness by hoarding the truth, as well as acting in a way that appears supernatural. This appeals to people who have a tendency to believe in.

* Paltering: speaking or acting in a way that confuses people and, as a result, diverts their attention away from them and towards you. In the end, you influence the attention of others to achieve your own goals. Magicians, conjurers and actors use this method.

4 Types of deception

Deception can be of two main types:

* Lying on commission (dissimulation) This is the main element of deception. In the case of lie by commission the person is deceived or deceives directly by intentionally altering material facts.

* Lying by omission (simulation) (also known as simulacrum): lying by omission is indirect. In this sense, the person committing the deception does not intend to alter the facts. Rather, the person consciously and intentionally conceals important facts of which he or she is aware and which could have affected the deceived person's choice.

Duperio

Deception is a form of deceit. However, it is aimed at selfishly benefiting the victim. When deception is involved, the offender sets traps or bait in which the victim is lured into falling and then takes advantage of them for unfair or illegal gain.

1. Indoctrination

Indoctrination consists of teaching someone an idea without giving them the opportunity to think critically.

2- Indoctrination strategies:

* Rote training: is the process of embedding information in people's minds through repetition. For example, saying a specific prayer phrase, as well as counting the beads when praying.

* Affirmation: having people say phrases that affirmatively support certain statements. In this way, they are taught to accept these statements as true.

* Spreading lies and facts. This is an intentional method of making the people being taught not have access to sources of truth or factual information. For example, they may be forbidden to read certain books that are considered "satanic". The use of fear psychology is often used, for example, telling people that they might experience nightmares or encounter vampire spirits in their sleep if they read such books.

* Let's face it, everyone has a "sinful" history. We all have skeletons in our past...the things we have done that we are ashamed of. One indoctrination strategy is to get people to confess. Once they have confessed, they lose their moral authority to stand up to the instructors. This means they become more submissive to instruction.

* Isolation - - the main objective of isolation is to remove individuals from any influence that might make indoctrination unattainable or difficult to achieve. Victims are isolated from their family, society or other normal relationships. It is

a type of denial of truth and truthfulness as the victims are unable to discern a different opinion about the claims made by the instructors.

* Imposition of guilt: Imposition of guilt is closely related to coerced confession. In guilt imposition, a feeling of guilt is induced in the victim's mind. The victim could be in a trap to commit a sin and the indoctrinator will find a way to uncover it. The indoctrinator takes advantage of that action to make the victim feel guilty. victim. The main objective, like forced confessions, is to diminish the moral status of the victim and thus force him/her into a state of psychological submission.

* The imposition of the phobia is a psychological fear. Indoctrinators instill fear in their victims to the point that they feel unable to live outside the confines of their indoctrinator. For example, the victim may be told of the "devil's" plan to destroy him, and the only way to be saved is to leave the demon-infested home and reside with the indoctrinator, who is capable of eliminating the evil one. There are various forms of phobia enforcement. For example, insurance companies inflict fear on their customers by exaggerating the risk that could arise if the customer chooses not to cover the lives of loved ones or the property of. They also target their citizens by instilling fear, especially when they want their own agenda to be dominant.

Rituals and rituals can be a powerful influence on an individual's psychology. This is why many religious practices, cults, traditions or political organizations and some civil organizations have rituals. For example, it is typical to perform rituals before prayer, before burials, before conflicts, and so on. Rituals can increase a person's susceptibility to certain ideas promoted by the teacher.

* Induced dependency, also known as induced dependency, is often used by manipulators in a situation to establish superiority over their victim. For example, imperialist or colonialist organizations may perpetuate poverty in the society they are targeting and then appear as saviors of that society. They can offer conditional aid, conditional subsidies, etc... and with conditions designed to make the recipients more vulnerable to being exploited. Because, without that intentional poverty, that particular society would not be in a position to be vulnerable or not to have embraced the conditional aid or subsidy, which is then a source of dependency. When couples are married it is typical for the insecure spouse to provoke a situation that makes the other dependent. For example, an insecure husband may cause his wife to lose her job. When the wife loses her job and the husband is insecure, the husband has total control of the non-working wife because he is the primary breadwinner. The woman's inability to earn a living means that she is more exposed to the husband's demands.

* Punishment - through a system of examinations including tests and quizzes, and also by offering incentives to those who complete the indoctrination course.

3 Characteristics of the indoctrination process.

It is not surprising that indoctrination occurs throughout our lives. It occurs at home (by parents), in our schools (by teachers), as well as in public life (by government officials and politicians), etc.

Here are some of the main characteristics of the techniques used to teach:

* Fear
* Dogmatism
* Fundamentalism
* Cognitive closure
Feeling of unworthiness
* Perception of deprivation

4 Sources of education

Although there are several hidden sources of information These are some of the most common sources of education:

* Religious institutions
* Educational centers and schools
* Media Main media, alternative media and social media
* Parents
* Politicians
* Marriage partners

Brainwashing

Brainwashing is the process of removing from a person's belief system the existing set of beliefs and replacing it with a new set of beliefs. It is done without anyone's consent.

Although sometimes brainwashing can be non-voluntary and subtle, most of the time it is violent. As an example, we have witnessed forced conversions in the crusade and when fighting in the jihad. When forced conversions are resorted to, the victims are aware that they are being brainwashed, but accept it as a strategy to avoid further risk of harm, such as death.

Brainwashing with violence is common in militant cults

or criminal groups, where victims are locked up and have no escape route.

Potential victims of brainwashing with violence could be:

* Privates (especially prisoners of war).

* Slaves in captivity

* Abducted victims

* Illegal aliens

When brainwashing is subtly occurring, the victim often willingly and unknowingly consents to the brainwashing. In this scenario, the perpetrator seeks victims who are more pliable. Victims are often in desperate situations and, therefore, have a psychological gap that is begging to be filled.

Here are just a few of the potential victims of brainwashing by uninformed people:

* Patients suffering from unidentified chronic illnesses.

Minors who have moved out of their home and live alone and often far away

* People who have lost their jobs and are devastated

* People who have lost loved ones, especially through death or divorce

Five common steps to brainwashing

Here are some of the steps commonly used by brainwashers to get their victims brainwashed:

Isolation

Attack on self-esteem

Subjugation

Testing

Love bombing

Isolation

The brainwasher understands that someone's family or circle of friends will observe what is happening and help the victim. So the first step they take is to separate the victim from their family and close friends.

Some, like the cult leader, are able to instill negative attitudes towards close family members and close friends. This can cause a rift between the victim and his or her loved ones and lead to feelings of isolation. For example, an occult leader may declare that your best acquaintance is a psychic vampire who drains your energy and makes you sick and that you should avoid that person. Since you are suffering and are desperate and despairing, you are likely to use this method of brainwashing and consequently separate yourself from the person who could have prevented you from being brainwashed.

Attack on self-esteem

The single victim who has self-doubt or self-esteem issues and generally low self-esteem is easily subjected to brainwashing. In this way, the brainwasher attempts to create this condition within the victim through a smear attack on the victim's self-esteem.

The ways in which the brainwasher attacks the victim's self-esteem include:

* Physical and verbal violence - which is commonly used in brainwashing that is violent, where the brainwasher makes use of abuse to make the victim feel inferior in order to make them lose their self-esteem.

* Lack of sleep - those who do not sleep are more likely to be subjected to the pressure of the mind due to the absence of

mindfulness. It is much easier for a person who is sleeping to follow the brainwashing patterns to relax and rest.

* Intimidation-Intimidation is one of the tactics employed by brainwashers to push someone into involuntary submission. For example, the threat of punishment is a form of intimidation.

Shaming - This is most often used when the victim is hiding an unpleasant secret that he or she does not want revealed. For example, the brainwasher may employ techniques to get nude photos of a potential victim, or trick the victim into a relationship that is not sexy. Once the brainwasher gets the information, he or she begins a subliminal effort to shame the victim. In this subliminal shaming the brainwasher does not reveal these materials to the public, but uses general phrases that suggest morality on the part of the victim. The victim may know where the signals lead and does everything possible to dissuade the brainwasher from revealing the embarrassing information. This gives the brainwasher an advantage that is used to control the victim's brain. For example, the person may be forced to perform rituals that erode the victim's self-esteem and self-worth and become a slave to the brainwasher. In the end, the victim may become ill with this Stockholm syndrome, in which the victim instead of fighting the brainwasher, acts to defend him or her - an act that subconsciously is more concerned with safeguarding those "secrets" (embarrassing information).

* Creation of scarcity, such as rationing of basic necessities, and then released after the victim's act.

Subjugation

Brainwashers try to put them under total control, so that they are completely obedient.

These are just some of the strategies used to subjugate:
* Extreme abuse
* Us versus them
* Love bombing

Extreme abuse

The victim suffers severe violence. Most often psychological and emotional abuse is used. Physical abuse is used only in violent brainwashing. Physical abuse is not used for subtle brainwashing.

Us versus them

The victim is coerced into choosing between the brainwasher and others. However, the person is not given the choice to leave.

The victim is introduced to other people who have already been brainwashed and allowed to praise the brainwasher. If the victim believes in "them" (the outside world) as a possible option The victim continues to be subjected to many punishments until he/she gets the ultimate option of becoming part of "us" and, in the end, becoming one of the brainwashed subjects.

Testing

Tests are conducted to determine if the victim made the "we" decision and does not wish to be part of "them". Testing is also used to determine the level of respect for the law.

Sometimes, under the cover of covert secret control, a victim may be granted freedom to be handed over to "them" (the rest of humanity) on the condition that he or she returns at a certain time. The victim is then checked to see if the victim wants to return to "us" (the group of brainwashed people).

If the victim does not want to return to "us", then he or she is kidnapped and returned to the fold, where the vicious circle begins.

On the other hand, if the victim decides to return to "us," they are transferred to the next stage, which is love bombing.

Most of the time, due to the isolation and induced dependency, even when the victim wants to reunite with "them", the person experiences a long recovery process and prefers to return to "us" rather than start the process all over again and rebuild the life that was lost.

Love Bombing

When tests are conducted and the results show that the victim has been successfully brainwashed, love bombing is used to get the victim to join the group. It can take the form of praise promotions naming the subject, receiving gifts, etc.

Dark seduction

Dark seduction is the use of psychologically obscure techniques to entice someone to enter into an agreement that serves their personal interests, but without benefit to the seduced.

A dark seducer manipulates the victim's desires to satisfy his or her own. Although seduction is often linked to the opposite gender, it is also identical to the same gender and sexual orientation. Dark seduction is not always about sexuality, but about the use of sexual arousal to achieve certain goals.

If a person is sexually seduced and manipulated, the victim

is less rational and less logical and therefore more vulnerable to manipulative behavior.

Here are some of the techniques used to seduce women in dark ways:

* Love bombing
* Erotic expressions
* Erotic expressions
* Gifts
* Sexual advances

The main objective of dark seduction lies in its ability to draw attention to the primitive Id within each person and diminish the effects of anti-cathexis. The victim is able to move away from his super-ego, and thus down to the basic level of the Id which is where hedonism is found.

The actions and rewards of arousal are imposed on the victim to reinforce the Id status and totally destroy the self-defense and common sense of the cathexis. Most of the time brainwashing and indoctrination can be used to aid in the destruction of the super-ego.

Hypnotization

Hypnotization consists of creating a state of non-receptive vulnerability, which is completely open to suggestions. The hypnotized person resembles the sleepwalker, who is primarily focused on walking and is completely oblivious to the signals coming from the world.

When in the state of hypnotism the person who has been hypnotized is unable to make references to sources outside the body and only draws references from suggestions. The person may largely or completely lose awareness of the peripheral.

This means that the mind is enclosed in a kind of conscious bubble that is completely inaccessible to any signals from outside consciousness.

1. **Hypnotic induction**

   Hypnotic induction is the process of using an initial set of instructions and suggestions designed to lure people into a state of hypnosis.

   The most important characteristics of hypnosis are:

   * Focused attention on an idea or object

   * Isolation of peripheral vision.

   * Increased receptivity to suggestions.

2. **Dark vs. white hypnosis**

   The distinction between white and dark hypnosis lies in the hypnotist's intention. Dark hypnosis is intended to take advantage of hypnosis to obtain a benefit for the person who is the hypnotist.

   White hypnosis is intended to improve the health of the hypnotized person, helping him or her to free themselves from an unrelenting or detrimental state of mind.

   Hypnotherapy is the most popular type using white hypnosis. White hypnosis is commonly described as therapeutic hypnosis.

3 Hypnotherapy

Hypnotherapy can be described as a method of hypnotic induction using white light by medical professionals for therapeutic purposes. The goal of the therapy is to help a patient heal from emotional, psychological, or emotional trauma as well as physical trauma.

Hypnotherapy is a method of pain relief as it allows the patient to separate from the cause of the pain, thus reducing sensitivity to the pain.

The facts about hypnosis:

It is a voluntary choice

* It is voluntary

Children are also more prone to hypnotism than adults.

15% of people are at risk of being hypnotized * A mere 10% could be controlled very well.

A mere 10% could be very rarely controlled.

* People who have trouble maintaining concentration in dreams are more susceptible to hypnotism.

Positive effects of dark induction hypnosis

There are numerous victims of dark induction hypnosis. These are the main causes of dark induction of hypnosis.

* Being hypnotized to the point of being willing to give your possessions to the one hypnotizing you.

The trick is to make you believe that you are obliged to let burglars in.

The trick is to make you feel hypnotized to the point that you are willing to go with the kidnappers to their hiding place

Chapter 4: Tools of dark and white psychology

Previously we have talked about "dark" and white as far as psychology is concerned. The next chapter will focus on the latter. We will examine the mind-shaping techniques that can be used in both areas. As with any tool, how it is used will depend on the purpose for which it is intended to be used.

A hoe is a useful tool that can provide you with a healthy harvest, but it can also be used to murder and maim.

An axe may help you have enough firewood to cook your favorite meal in a remote camp, but it could be used to steal or commit murder.

Nuclear materials can be used as a cheap source of energy, as well as for the treatment and diagnosis of disease, but they can also be used to build a genocidal atomic bomb.

It all depends on the mind.

These are the main mind-shaping tools (or mind-based models) that we will examine:

Mindfulness meditation

Neurolinguistic programming

Neuroplasticity

Power posture

Positive affirmation

Creative visualization

Depending on your particular needs and goals, these are general tools that can help you:

Get rid of your dark psychological habits.

* Develop an autoimmune perspective against the dark side of psychological problems.

- Increase your awareness in dark psychological detection.

Increase your ability to use the positive aspects of the

dark to your advantage.

Mindfulness meditation

In hypnotism, we have noted the importance of intense concentration to a specific concept or object is used to induce hypnotic behavior. Meditation is appropriate for hypnotic induction, but it can also be used to perform other forms of dark psychology, such as brainwashing, indoctrination and deception, as well as seduction.

Meditation is from the beginning of time to help people achieve a higher level of concentration. That is why it is a tool that can be used in white psychology or dark psychology depending on the purpose.

1- What is meditation?

Meditation is the act of returning to the state of being in which one's awareness of oneself is greater. When you practice meditation it is possible to free yourself from patterns that have become part of your mind to allow you to go about your day. When you meditate, you are able to reconnect with your inner self and reflect on your inner self.

2. What is mindfulness?

Mindfulness is the state of being aware of the present moment and in a non-judgmental, loving and attentive manner that is unaffected by judgment.

According to this definition, the value of mindfulness is greater for white psychology than for dark psychology. It can be used as an effective tool against the hypnotic effect of darkness. Moreover, in a state of mindfulness you can easily detect deception, indoctrination, brain-washing and even seduction. This could make you less prone to people who want to employ them on you.

3. What is the relationship between meditation and mindfulness?

The act of meditation is a method of practice that is intended to help achieve mindfulness. The state of mindfulness is that which is achieved through meditation.

Therefore, mindfulness meditation can be described as a form of meditation that aims to achieve the state of mindfulness.

4. The Purpose of Mindfulness Meditation Practice

The purpose of mindfulness practice is to experience the present moment in its entirety. Living life to the fullest refers to:

* Living fully in the present, without assigning the totality of your life to either the past or the future.

* Being aware of your life and how you live it so that none of it is wasted when you become attached to the past or create attachments to the future.

* Fully allowing yourself to be in the present moment, without putting too much emphasis on it.

The ability to experience each moment without attaching to any identity or identity. If you connect to something, the experience disappears into the past.

5 Improve your concentration by meditating.

If you are dissatisfied with the amount of concentration you are experiencing or want to focus your attention on greater and higher quality goals than you have thought about, contemplate the practice of meditation.

Here are some of the ways you can increase your concentration by meditating:

* Understand the meaning of concentration. Concentration is the act of directing your attention, focus and attention away from distractions to focus on the most important aspect of your life in the present moment.

* Decide your area of concentration. The things you focus on shape your personality. It is not uncommon to meet long-married couples who look like a sister and brother. Children of multiple parents joined in the same household begin to share some distinctive physical traits. What happens when certain people are able to somehow aesthetically (at least in the mind) begin to resemble your hobbies, favorite cars, favorite pets, favorite projects, etc.? Concentration. Therefore, the object of your concentration plays an important role in determining who you are. It is a power of re-creation!

Be a witness to those who participate in it. Many religions, particularly Christianity, try to be a witness to the truth, which are the events during the time of the event. This is the most effective method to learn to realize it. Observe others concentrating.

Avoid distractions. If you need to be tidy, then you must get rid of the dirt. If you are trying to concentrate, you must be careful about multitasking. This is as beneficial when you meditate as it is in any profession or specialty. Stay away from distractions, avoid dirty minds, stay away from moving images, avoid smells, and keep objects away from your fingers.

Focus your attention and practice mindfulness in your daily tasks. Practice makes perfect. Don't wait for the moment of meditation to focus your attention. Try to do it as often as you can throughout all your activities.

Be at peace. The goal of calmness is to reduce the amount of energy you spend on distractions and instead allow it to be used to maintain your peace. This can help increase the clarity of your concentration.

Six tips to improve your meditation

Anyone can use one or two tips to improve the quality of their meditation. This is especially applicable to those just beginning the practice.

The most effective way to increase your knowledge about something is to have the relevant information at your fingertips. This will help you tap into the reservoir of knowledge whenever necessary. Meditation is no exception.

Here are the most important suggestions to help you improve your meditation skills:

Select the meditation technique that you like (that you feel comfortable with).

Don't try to force the mechanics.

Figure out what you want to get out of your meditation.

Avoid procrastination

Don't have expectations

Find the best time for you

Find a specific place for meditation (a kind of temple)

Don't focus on the quantity of meditation time, but on the quality

Find the right posture for meditation.

Closing your eyes or leaving them open when meditating are different options, each with its own benefits. Closed eyes can help ensure deep meditation. Open eyes help ensure that you are in tune with your surroundings when meditating. Therefore, neither is good.

There is no particular meditation method that is superior to another. Whatever works for you is best.

Neuro Linguistic Programming (NLP)

Neuro Linguistic Programming (NLP), as the name implies, comprises three fundamental components:

Neurology

Language

Programming

Neurology is a word derived from the word "neuro. The word "neuro" comes directly from neurology. It is the Greek term "neuron" which is used to describe nerves. The suffix "logy" is a derivative of the Greek word 'logia', which is simply a synonym for 'study'. Thus, we can define neurology as the study of nerves. But in the scientific sense, it is classified as a medical field that focuses on the treatment and diagnosis of any disease that is directly or indirectly related to neurology.

Language is a human communication system that employs one, several or all forms of expression, such as the use of gestures, writing or speech, to convey emotions or inner thoughts and to understand complex and abstract thinking. Language is crucial in enabling us to communicate with each other in order to satisfy our wants and needs, and to build and maintain relationships with as well as our culture and traditions.

Programming refers to the process or procedure of establishing certain patterns of behavior.

Programming is the mystical glue that connects Neuro and Linguistics. When combined with Neuro-Linguistics, it opens up an even greater dimension that is beyond all the toxins of the brain. Free your mind from its prison by building the map of an ideal path to freedom of the mind.

The basic definitions of the key concepts allow us to unravel the essence of NLP implies. NLP is the practice and science that is primarily concerned with the research and study of how individuals organize their thoughts, feelings communication and behavior to produce their desired outcomes.

Simply put, we can say that NLP helps us dissect the link between the way we think (neuro) and how we express the thoughts we have (linguistic), as well as the pattern that governs our behavior and emotions (programs).

The fundamental idea of NLP

The fundamental idea of NLP is that people create their own visual maps of the environment due to the method by which they filter and process the information captured by the five senses. In this sense, the word "neuro" has a distinct meaning - it is a reference to the mental map that originates from an individual's distinct mental filtering system that processes the information captured through his or her five senses. The mental map can comprise components such as smells, sounds, tastes, internal images and awareness that flesh out the basis of a person's neurological filtering process. In NLP terms, the mental map is often referred to as the "first access".

Like neuro, linguistics has a meaning unique to NLP and

is simply the assignment of personal meanings to information gathered from the environment. The linguistic process fills in this Linguistic Map by assigning language to tastes, smells, emotions, sounds and internal images, leading to higher consciousness. The Linguistic Map is the second map of NLP.

NLP is all about mind mapping. In reality, every journey you take is taking steps along the path your mind maps out in front of your feet. You cannot walk voluntarily without having a mental plan. You may be doing this action subconsciously, and you may not be aware of it, but you are.

The basics of NLP

NLP revolves around three essential aspects:

Subjectivity is how each of us perceives the world from a different perspective.

Maps are our personal worlds consisting of boundaries and areas that our daily experiences define for us. Maps are the only representation of a place, not the actual place.

Language has the ability to change and redefine boundaries with our control systems, one of which is language.

The basic concepts of NLP to know are:

* The models that other people have of the world are not necessarily correct.

* The essence of communication is in the reaction it generates.

* Everyone does the best he/she can using the resources he/she has available.

You have the power of your mind, and consequently its outcome.

* Individuals are not the cause of their actions, nor are they related to them.

The 6 most important NLP tools to improve relationships

NLP is more a set of tools than a tool. It is a workshop. There are a variety of tools in this NLP workshop.

Because Dark Psychology is more concerned with relationships, it is possible to use numerous NLP tools that can be used in the context of relationships. The following are six key NLP tools that can be used to manage various relationships:

Anchor

Dissociation and association

Agreement frame

Reframing

Rapport

Belief change

Anchoring

Anchoring is the act of fixing an internal reaction to an external or internal trigger. The objective of anchoring is to

* To focus attention on the consciousness

* Re-access cognitive information and internal state

* Linking experiences to enhance meaning and consolidate information

* Transfer experiences and learning to other environments.

Signals are crucial to establishing an anchor. Successful anchoring requires the ability to connect a cue to those instances where the information can be quickly linked to an enhancing internal state. There are two methods of establishing the association:

* Repetition is the process of creating the constant connection between stimulus and response through repetition. In essence, it is a continuous reinforcement of the anchor.

* Intense connection - connecting an intense mental state with a specific stimulus.

Anchors with well-formed conditions

Anchors with well-formed conditions is the term used to describe the conditions necessary for an anchor to function. This includes:

* The intensity and quality of the response

* The uniqueness of the stimulus being used as an anchor

* The timing and pairing of the stimulus and the response

* The context of the anchoring experience

To develop anchors that are effective

Figure out what state you want your loved one to be in. It can be joy and courage, or empathy or any other.

* Use every means to allow the person to be in a similar state.

* When your loved one reaches the desired state, you can hug him or her for a few minutes and remember the place where you have held him or her.

* Remove your hands from the person and speak to him or her in a way that dissociates the subject from the person who is the subject

* After a few minutes, contact the person again in exactly the same place as before and observe the response. If the person responds in the same way, you will know that your anchoring has worked. If not, you can find a suitable time to repeat the procedure, using a different location.

Association and dissociation

The concepts of "association" and dissociation are similar to light and darkness. One is a necessity in the absence of the other. Life is a process of alternation between the two, i.e., the process of creation and decay. The term "association" refers to mixing, bundling and bundling together, combining, etc. Dissociation is defined by isolating, segregating and dividing.

It is defined as paying attention to the present moment by paying attention to everything around you; being aware, listening and experiencing the action occurring in the present. In reference to memory or imagination, eliminating any past or future events in the present moment; seeing and hearing as if you were in the present moment.

Dissociation can be described as the act of withdrawing your awareness from the space of the self so that you are able to see and experience the self as an unbiased observer. This means that you will be able to evaluate your self-image as an outsider would. This allows you to change your identity without being influenced by the needs of your self.

However, in relationships it is possible to use dissociation to dissociate your loved ones or partner from negative, unpleasant or disempowering situations and beliefs. If, for example, you are discussing problems or difficulties, try to keep your loved ones out of the discussion.

Both Association and Dissociation have their own signs.

Some of the most common associations are:

* "you," "we," "us," "us," and "this."
* Using a person's name: "John, read this" * Indicating the present moment: "John, read this".

* Indicating the present moment: "as you are currently experiencing it...", or "as you are currently experiencing it...".

* Spatially enclosing listeners in the context of: "as you are experiencing it at this moment..."

* Talking and asking about something as if it were real using words like "because" or "of course."

* Gestures that signal that it is present in or on the person's body or even within their aura.

* Related sensory cues "hear by your own ears", "see with your own eyes", "feel with your body", etc.

Some of the most common dissociation cues are:

* Referring to "he", "he", "she", "it", "they", "someone", "one", "a person" and "it" in representations.

* Referring to the listener, or the group to which he or she belongs, by names that do not reflect the listener or the group, e.g., pseudonyms.

- Projecting current events into the future or past E.g., "you were a pro at this."

Distinguish the listener from the image spatially: "how do you hear and feel those human beings there"

* Making use of hypothetical examples such as, "if you saw an antelope playing the guitar"

* Using sensory cues to indicate separation "as it is possible to see the pond, notice how far away it appears to be" * Using gestures to suggest that the antelope is playing the guitar.

Using gestures to suggest that something referred to is far away, such as when describing the distance to a particular place by imitating a tired walk.

Frame of agreement

This is a subliminal method in which you don't need to completely agree with the person's point of view, but you don't want the person to be upset. An agreement frame usually contains the following main ingredients:

I agree

I am respectful

I appreciate

It is used to indicate that you agree in your response to indicate that you agree with someone's point of view and (not "but") you would like to add your own opinion about it.

It is acceptable to use the word "respect" in your response when you want to acknowledge another person's point of view, even if you disagree with it.

It is appropriate to use the word "appreciation" in your response when you find nothing in another person's perspective that you disagree with or don't consider, but still want to respect the other person's point of view.

Sounds simple, doesn't it? However, most people don't get it. We are so focused on who is right and who is wrong that, more often than not, we fail to take note of the details of the conversations we are having. It's not uncommon for us to feel that we don't value our interlocutors. Add to the mix a few emotions and nerves and there you have a new discussion. Most human conflict is ignited by small sparks that fly from the simplest things.

Reframing

If you live through an experience you don't like, if you pay attention and carefully, you will discover that what you dislike is not the sensation itself, but your reaction to it. For example, if you suffer from malaria and you are handed a bottle whose contents and label say quinine syrup (an extremely bitter medicine) you may take that bitter syrup with a smile. What happens if, for example, the same quinine syrup is put into a container that looks like an ice cream jar labeled "Honey" and you decide to think it is honey? Your first reaction is to throw it away in disgust. Yes, same sensory experience, however, different responses. So, in this case, it's quinine syrup that has been transformed by using a jar of honey as a label. It's the same thing that happens when you have a piece of artwork that you don't find appealing. When you put the artwork in an additional frame, you suddenly begin to be captivated by it. Why? It's because it has been "reframed" in a new way.

That's how you can alter the reaction to quinine syrup, or to a work of art by changing the label and the bottle or reframing the artwork, and also, you can alter people's reaction to a particular experience by placing the experience in a different context. So, if you can alter the meaning of an experience for another person, you can also alter their reactions to it.

The following are the basic steps necessary for effective reframing:

Try to improve your sense of hearing by practicing. When interacting with the subject to access the experience, try their language structures, as well as their physical state. ocular access cues, as well as nonverbal analogues (body language).

Think your thoughts before you speak. It is important to observe the person's perspective and create a reframe that, when delivered, has the right impact on the individual. To create a successful reframe, try to design your frame as the exact opposite of the person's current experience.

- If you are conducting a formal (non-conversational) reframing, help the person develop a rich internal representation (auditory, visual, kinesthetic) of the "problematic" experience by associating fully with it. You can also ask the client to replay the experience of the "problem" so that you can fully connect with it, which will help maximize the impact of the message when you present it. This will also allow you to refine your reframing.

- Make sure you present your reframing congruently (so that no conflicts occur).

- Practice sensory acuity after delivery to determine if the patient reacts differently upon seeing the "problem" behavior.

- Be persistent. Always test and pace your reframing to make sure the effects don't wear off. If you don't, you may cause the person to revert to the previous responses before reframing.

There are two main types of reframing: reframing content and context. Both are very important in the context of connections.

Context reframing

Context reframing is the process of taking a "problem or experience that is in a context in which it appears to be 'problematic and then placing it in a setting in which it no longer becomes a problem or the experience is capable of having an effect that is beneficial or positive, or is a benefit or skill that is useful. Context reframing recognizes that there is no incorrect sensory representation, but only an appropriate or incorrect context.

Let's look, for example, at how the following three statements can be contextualized.

It moves so slowly

The smartphone is priced too high.

It is too demanding.

Before altering the meaning of these statements, consider asking yourself:

At a snail's pace for what reason?

What is the difference?

Stingy according to whom?

If you try to answer these questions, be sure to ask yourself what other context in which this characteristic or behavior is found might be considered more appropriate or useful as a talent or asset.

The most contextually appropriate reframes for the above statements could be

He works at the speed of a snail - and when you're engrossed in his intricate and inventive work, you'll know why there are hundreds of orders waiting to be filled.

The smartphone is expensive - I'd love to consider a less expensive model, at 30% less, that will last a tenth of this. this is definitely the most affordable offering I've ever seen!

It's very tight - and that's the exact way you've managed to buy an extravagant home.

Content reframing.

Unlike with context reframing, with content reframing, the context remains the same, but the meaning of the context is altered and consequently the responses we receive are altered.

For example, you just got divorced. Instead of getting depressed and angry, and feeling that you are wasting the time and money you have spent on your relationship, you look at the positive aspect of the situation by focusing on the possibilities that a new relationship offers, as well as the new adventure associated with it, and the need to mend your ways again.

There are many other examples of how content reframing can be used in everyday life. For example:

* Affirmation "Oh, this driver speeds. He shouldn't be driving. I don't like drivers who speed too much.

* Reframed content such as: I imagine that driver is driving the emergency car. He could save a lot of lives if he became an ambulance driver. He could also prevent a lot of houses from burning down if he were a fire truck driver.

* Statement: It's very troublesome. I don't like trouble.

* Content rephrased as: problems are not just challenges. They are opportunities to learn new skills, opportunities to improve our actions, and opportunities to learn.

* Statement: He is too lazy. Would rather come up with a method for not doing something rather than doing it. I don't like laziness.

Reframing content as laziness gives us the opportunity to discover more efficient ways to expend less effort and focus our energy on the issues that need our attention the most.

Content reframing can be used effectively in response to cause-and-effect statements (whenever A happens, I respond with Z). It can also be used to address the complicated concept of equivalence, whereby one thing can be interpreted in different ways.

To create effective content reframing, it is essential to think about questions such as.

What has this individual not noticed in the same way that might reveal new meaning and alter the person's reaction?

What aspect of the facts is outside of this person's perspective/awareness that when he or she is aware will cause him or her to see things differently?

What else might this behavior mean?

Rapport

Rapport is an essential method of connecting with all types of people. There are a variety of ways to create rapport with people are:

- Discreetly observing the person's breathing patterns.
* Refrain from revealing their body language
* Using the same terms as the person in a differentiated way
* Understanding and using the person's senses.

In terms of sensory perception there are three primary sensory perceptions you can observe from a person based on how the individual uses language to communicate with others:

* Visual - those who have a sensory perception that is visual tend to use phrases that refer to "vision" such as "my eyes are sharp", "I understand the meaning you are trying to convey and your futuristic future seems bright", and words such as "see", "imagine", color "clear", "hazy", "envision appearing" perspective. They also often describe shape using terms such as "see small," "light brown," "rectangular," etc.

* Auditory: those who perceive their sensory experience as auditory often make use of phrases that refer to hearing such as "I can hear you", "he scratched the floor and his voice was clear" "I am listening to you" and words such as "listen", "talk" and "discuss" """""" call, etc. They also describe the form in terms of the word "listen", e.g., loud beeps, "loud or "ticking", etc.

* Kinesthetic: those with kinesthetic sensory perceptions often use phrases such as "I think this is the best way to achieve this", "my feelings do not support this", "she is very welcome", "I feel this", "I am unable to understand this", or "I am afraid of this", as well as phrases such as "feel the touch", "be afraid", "warm", "cold", "rough", "soft", etc.

Change of beliefs

How much love can you give?

This is a question most couples ask themselves during their relationships. Before addressing this question, you probably have to ask yourself "enough for what exactly?". You would probably answer with another question, "How many years of love is enough to ensure that my relationship is stable and allows me to enjoy the happiness I desire and experience the way I want to feel myself?" Does this now help you answer this question?

The issue is not just love as a whole, but your goals and objectives. If you are not able to find enough love to satisfy your desires, goals and objectives, then something is holding you back.

NLP can help you ask simple but powerful questions. It is possible to ask yourself "If I am not able to feel enough love, what is holding me back?". This question can lead you to the Pandora's box that contains the root of your worries, fears or conflicts.

Some of the concerns about love are, "I don't have enough love because I am afraid I am not worthy of it," "I don't have enough love because I am afraid of getting entangled in it and losing my freedom," "I am afraid it will make me lose my identity," "Love is blind and can make me feel manipulated." All of these statements are classified as limiting beliefs, that is, beliefs that restrict your ability to achieve what you are capable of doing. Limiting beliefs prevent you from achieving the success and prosperity you desire.

Believer Change is a method that helps you identify the beliefs that limit you and conquer negative beliefs. If you follow this procedure it is possible to explore your mind and discover the limiting beliefs that are within your subconscious mind, which prevent you from achieving the things you want from your life. Through this process it is possible to overcome limitations with new and more powerful belief systems.

The most common beliefs about relationships fall into three broad categories:
* The belief in a cause.
* The belief system about the meaning of a word.
* Personal beliefs about identity.

In order to have a satisfying relationship one must eliminate any limiting assumptions. The most common beliefs are "all men are sexually adulterous" and "all men are dogs and women are annoying and all women are smart", etc. These are negative beliefs that prevent you from fully and completely enjoying your relationship. You will need to modify these beliefs to fully enjoy and appreciate your relationship.

The six tools mentioned above are effective in making your relationship satisfying and fulfilling.

Is NLP a totally white or dark tool for psychology?

NLP is a flexible tool. It is a tool that can be used in both dark and white psychology. It is a powerful tool for both.

Most people who practice dark psychology use many NLP tools. Therefore, if you want to engage in dark psychology, it is essential that you learn NLP. However, when you are trying to combat dark psychology, it is essential to be aware of the basics of NLP.

NLP as a dark psychological tool

NLP is a popular tool for influencing people with dark persuasion and brainwashing, seduction, the use of hypnosis, and on a larger scale, for psychological manipulation.

Understanding NLP can help in understanding how this tool can be employed in the formulation of these dark psychology techniques.

20 NLP as a white psychological tool

We will learn more about how to use NLP for a method of defense against dark psychology predators later in Part II.

Neuroplasticity

Neuroplasticity is the process of changing the wiring of the brain to free it from the brain lock. It is the process of rewiring the brain to free it from the lock. Schwartz, a renowned neuroscientist, created the well-known Four Ways process as a way of dealing with brain lock that includes mindfulness as one of the main elements.

Brain block can be described as a neurological condition in which the brain is locked in the state of being "on." It is like pressing the bell on a doorbell and having it stay in: it will keep ringing constantly even though you know you don't want it to ring. The brain block effect is most evident in those suffering from OCD. In this type of condition the patient repeats routine tasks such as frequently going to wash hands, regularly checking the door, just to verify that it is locked going to the bathroom even when there is no real need and so on.

In the brain, the thought that is in the "on" lock is blocked from continuing to appear repeatedly. The most effective method to combat brain lock is neuroplasticity.

Focused attention (concentration meditation) The most effective tool for neuroplasticity.

The subconscious mind is in the dark. If it is not illuminated by focused attention, it is in the dark. However, the power of focused attention will never cease to be intense, allowing it to penetrate to the very depths of the unconscious mind. What remains buried within the subconscious mind is transformed into a potential within the subconscious mind, and later transformed into kinetic energy in your conscious brain.

Powerful concentrated focus is evident in the physical world. Lenses are known to focus light energy. If this light power is directed to paper, it glows and burns. LASER (Light Amplification through Stimulated Expulsion of Radiation) is one of the best known physical technologies that is the result of the power of concentrated attention. Light is directed through the liquid medium along straight lines and bounces back due to the deflection of the prism wall. Each time the light bounces through the prism, it increases in intensity (is amplified). Laser light is known to cut diamonds and other hard metals. It makes incisions during surgery, and also cuts materials such as thick sheets of paper, metal foil and tissue into the required sizes. This is the power of concentrated focus!

It takes your subconscious mind as a transparent liquid to which knowledge of the external environment of your world is directed and then acquires more energy through the properties of your mind's subconscious so that, as time goes on, more and more high quality information emerges What a brilliant procedure! Light is energy. Your thoughts are just a small portion of vibrating energy. The amplification of light, regardless of prisms or lenses, is produced by the blasting or excitation of the ghosts within the light, resulting in more vibrations, and of greater magnitude. Your thoughts are also energy that are capable of being similarly excited and amplified to achieve a greater power that is simply the power, in fact, the power of thought!

The subconscious of your mind acts as this lens. Your subconscious is a laser prism. It is composed of properties that stimulate the energy of your thoughts to higher levels of vibration, thus creating more energy. It only requires your focused attention. Stories are told of Buddhist monks who can focus their attention on that crystal until it shatters and on the spoon until it bends. Miracles? Yes, they are possible when you are unaware of the power of focus. The power of this property, called "miracle," resides deep in the subconscious mind. It requires only one stimulus, directing your thoughts toward a higher quality over and over again until it can be strengthened. Learning is based on this basic idea. As you continue to read or review a subject, the better you understand and grasp its meaning. Why? Because your good idea constantly bounces back through the amplifying medium, the subconscious brain, continually increasing your energy levels.

Not using what you have learned

The most important concept of neuroplasticity is learned non-use. This means that the brain rewires itself to use less of a particular resource within the body.

For example, if a leg is disabled, the brain learns not to use it in everyday activities. The same happens when an eye, arm or ear has problems. It is also common for one side of your gum to hurt or for a tooth to ache. You will find that most of the time it is almost instinctive and you unconsciously choose the side that does not hurt to chew your food. At first, you may do this by mechanical means, but over time the brain is wired not to send instructions to the jaw muscles to make use of the side that is injured. In fact, the tongue is able to naturally partition food to the healthier side of the mouth for chewing.

Neuroplasticity as an obscure psychological tool

Although neuroplasticity is typically used as a white psychology tool, it can also be used as an alternative tool for dark psychology. We will explore how neuroplasticity can be used as a defense against dark psychology predators later in Part II.

The non-use learning technique can be used for brainwashing, indoctrination the use of hypnosis, and even seduction.

For example, through the process of brainwashing, an individual can be prevented from thinking critically or from reading from a specific selection of literary materials where truth and truth can be gleaned. In this Cold War period, it was normal in the Western world to discourage its citizens from reading material produced by the communists. Teachers, as well as lecturers and professors, were advised not to study such material or even talk about it. Thus, it was taught that communist material and concepts were not to be used.

At the same time, during the Cold War, both the Western and Eastern blocs engaged in indoctrination as a Cold War strategy. Each bloc tried to force its population to participate in not using, or learning about, the facilities or opportunities offered from the opposing bloc. "Us versus them" was the rallying cry in this non-use of learning. This meant that people were deterred from participating in the same method of critical thinking and were susceptible to being brainwashed by the propaganda machines employed by both sides of the bloc.

Power Posing

Power Posing, like NLP meditation practice as well as Neuroplasticity, can serve two purposes in its use as a tool. It is a tool that can be used as a dark psychological tool as well as a white psychological tool.

Before we dive into its different utilities, let's take a look at what it is.

What exactly is Power Posing?

Power posing is the art of positioning yourself in a way that conveys power.

The Powerful Purpose of Power

Power posing is not something you do just for the sake of it. It must be a deliberate (objective) act. These are the intentions of power:

* To get noticed

* To attract recognition

* To demonstrate competence

To gain a competitive advantage over other competitors *
To avoid risk of attack

* To avoid the risk of attack

The Science Behind Posing for Power

Posing for power is a public art. However, there are some internal factors that allow this to be possible. Social psychologists have shown that power poses have a huge impact on your personality, as well as emotional, mental and psychological impacts.

Power effects create a positive impact on your brain.

Power Posing can alter your brain chemistry by increasing testosterone (dominance hormone) and decreasing cortisol (stress hormone). This can make you feel more confident and secure.

Powerful effects that affect your emotions.

A high testosterone level, accompanied by lower cortisol levels boost your "feel good" effect which can help you get rid of or reduce negative moods.

The effects of being able to have on your mind

By increasing testosterone levels and therefore lowering

your stress levels, you are likely to feel more confident in facing challenges, confident in your worth and your self-esteem improves.

The most significant benefits of power

Posing with power can bring immense positive effects on your health. The amount of these benefits depends on the intention you set for yourself and the way you practice it.

Here are just a few of the most important benefits:

* A renewed inner self

* A great social standing

- A fulfilling career

* Indomitable bargaining power

A recognizable leadership ability

A resolute inner self

Research has shown that power poses don't just deliver external results. They actually have an impact on your inner self. Power poses work in a way that inspires and frees your self from a variety of toxic issues. Power posing helps to generate:

A fear-free self. Fear will be one of the biggest threats to your soul. It is a psychological disease that can cause dangerous results, including low self-confidence and self-doubt, low self-esteem, negative self-image and many more.

An inner self that is willing to accept the outer self. One of the most challenging personality conflicts is the conflict with your self-image and your outer self. Whatever your inner self looks like, but as long as your outer self does not appear powerful, positive and self-confident, your inner self will end up damaged and shattered by the negativity it receives from the outer self.

A remarkable social position

We are all social beings. Social interactions affect us in all areas. The good news is that we are also capable of significantly influencing society. How we shape society is determined by how we choose to live our lives. The most difficult task for each individual is to construct the kind of society we would like to live in. It is impossible to tackle this task if our social position is not that good. We need to have a high social position to influence society.

Posing with power can help you in this endeavor by allowing you:

* A status in society that is assertive. - Assertiveness can be defined as the ability to present your goals. Many people confuse assertiveness with aggressiveness. It is more aggressive in the sense of. It is about being polite but assertive in your cause without resorting to violence of any kind whether physical or mental.

A welcoming social status image by using power posing techniques such as open arms hugging, smiling and not intruding on the privacy of another's property increases your social status so as not to cause a negative reaction to the person you are talking to. This can create a feeling of friendliness and warmth.

A social standing that is prepared for obstacles - whenever you strike a pose, you send messages to everyone that you are willing to overcome any difficulty to achieve what is required.

Indomitable bargaining power

Many of us don't even realize that every day we engage in a discussion. Every conversation is a part of the negotiation, even if it's only a minute. Getting our side of the story accepted as fact and believed as such is, in essence, having achieved negotiation. When we were children at home we were taught to negotiate with our parents for gifts, dinner and various other cares. Negotiation skills improve and get stronger as we grow up. In the future, once we have graduated from college or university, we are expected to negotiate our salary and wages. How much we negotiate or whether or not we receive a raise will depend on how we have shown our influence to the prospective employer in a way that demonstrates that we are confident in our skills, our motivation and our ability to perform the job at hand.

This gives you invincible bargaining power that can take its shape:

- The ability to present yourself to get big deals: families, companies and nations are constantly looking for courageous people who can be their representatives during difficult negotiations. Therefore, by presenting yourself with power, you will be recognized as someone with the confidence and ability to negotiate for big deals.

* The ability to influence negotiations in your favor, whether they are business or diplomatic agreements, the power of posing becomes essential to grant you the upper hand. If you don't have the power to pose you will be seen as weaker by the opposing party and, as a result, the other party could leverage their position to feel more superior than they expect you to grow.

* The ability to pick it up big The higher the power, the bigger the pie. Human psychology is prone to reward people

who believe they are superior or more powerful than those who appear less powerful or superior. If you appear more powerful than your peers, you are likely to get more deals when it comes to negotiating.

The Unmistakable Power of Leadership

Leadership is the ability to influence others to achieve your goals. The exercise of influence requires the power to. To get people to follow your example you must be sure that you are willing, in a position to lead them. They have to be able to see it, think it, and feel it. Power poses can be very effective on people's imagination, vision and emotions.

To show unmistakable leadership ability it is essential to pose as:

You must stand out above others - It is often believed that "the law of averages" works for those who are average. If you want to avoid being considered average, the first step is to be above average. In the forest, the tallest tree is the most admired. Therefore, it is important to act in a way that stands out from others in order to be seen as a leader.

You must be able to attract attention When you make yourself stand out you attract the attention of others. However, to be recognized as a leader is all about how you reveal your body language. You have to be able to convey an empowered posture to earn the honor of being considered the title of leader.

Don't dominate your space If you shrink back, for example, by wrapping your arms around your chest or putting your foot on top of another and so on, it indicates that you are not capable of occupying your space (and most likely, a discreet invitation to intruders). If you have a wide stance, such as arms outstretched and legs set wide and a long stride when walking, in addition to other things, this indicates that you are capable of occupying your space, and using it to the fullest to take charge. Obviously, leadership is about controlling the space of others.

* You demonstrate your authority every time you raise your cheeks, enter a meeting with your legs out to the side when standing or with your feet on the floor in a seated position, you are effectively in the act of establishing your power. There are certain psychological signals that indicate to others that you are, in fact, an authority figure and that you are actually doing the authority.

Power posturing as an instrument of dark psychology.

Most manipulators employ power poses to dominate their subject. Power poses are often used by narcissists to control their subject.

Most manipulators use Power poses to appear powerful and make their subjects fear them.

The best method to see that Power uses its power is to observe the posturing of the most powerful leaders, particularly those with autocracy.

Posing in Power is a white psychological tool.

Posing in Power can be used to deter attempts by narcissistic individuals to take over your life. For example, the best method of defending yourself from a bully is to use power posing.

Power posing does not only take place in the personal realm. It is also a reality in the corporate world as well as on a global scale to aid domination in the military and economic realms.

Positive thinking and positive affirmations

Positive affirmations and positive thinking are very synergistic. Conversely, the opposite, i.e., negative affirmations and negative thinking are also synergistic.

Although positive affirmations and positive thinking are typical tools of white psychological research, they can also be used to aid dark psychology, in particular to increase the confidence and self-esteem of the manipulator.

Positive thinking, for example, is commonly used by marketing to increase sales. It is also used by politicians to motivate crowds. In this way, it can be employed as a tool of deception and propaganda. Positive thinking can also be used as a prelude to the hypnotic induction process.

When it comes to dark psychology, the use of positive thoughts and affirmations that are positive are employed to attract victims to the manipulator and gain their trust. Then trust and faith can be used to the detriment of the victim.

When it comes to rituals that are often used to psychologically influence affirmations cannot be missing. For example, prayers for religious or political purposes and slogans of organizations, etc., are basically affirmations. They can be positive as well as negative affirmations.

Positive thinking

Positive thinking is a mindset perspective that concentrates on the positive aspects of oneself and imagines the advantages that result from this type of thinking.

Positivism as a method to help white psychology.

The most important thing to know about life is that no one was created to be miserable. No one was created to have an unhappy life. We were all created to be happy and joyful. But due to a variety of factors beyond our reach, happiness, joy and success have been impossible because of the negativity that has enveloped our minds. But, within our minds lies the key to ignite optimism and happiness. All we need to do is start by focusing on the positive.

The first step is to consult the compass to find the direction to go. This is the only way to take a step that is not an endless wandering. The same thing happens in the mind. It is necessary to initiate thought. Thought must be based on a sense of what it is required to be. To positively initiate thought is to make the mind first understand what it is before giving it the proper direction, a positive direction.

In a world that is full of competition, and with success becoming a commodity at times, you can be overwhelmed if you do not meet the criteria that are the price of this popular success. Success has become a commodity whose value is determined by how much it is worth in terms of money. This makes many of those who are unsuccessful in the marketplace unhappy and feel negative about themselves, and sometimes about everything around them.

Positive thinking can bring the original sense of accomplishment. It is a success that is not measured by momentary gains. It is a success that is unique enough that it cannot be measured in a context or on a measurement scale. It is in this unique feeling of achievement that we can discover our true essence - the place where we discover that we are uniquely and wonderfully made and that we are able to use all the potential we have within us to fulfill our individual goals in this world.

Positive thinking allows you to unleash the best of yourself that you can be a part of humanity. If you are not optimistic, your desire to achieve will be stifled. Positive thinking boosts your confidence and increases your motivation to pursue and realize your potential.

Positive affirmations

Positive affirmations are positive, personal statements that reveal your identity, who you are and should be in the present moment.

Therefore, positive affirmations take the form of a present tense because they are not framed around what you will become in the future, but what you are currently as you should be.

The positive affirmation follows the principle that "what you believe is what you will become." Therefore, you try to affirm the best part of you, the way you should be, by the way you speak. Your mind is forced to focus on your own words, and work with them instead of retreating into the darkness of negative thoughts. In this way it is easy to see the ways in which NLP strategies can be used for positive affirmations.

Understand why you need affirmations to be positive.

Many people don't understand how the brain works. The mind depends on a program stored in your memory that is deeply embedded in your memory. Your mind relies heavily on this program (mental model) to understand the present. This mental model (mental map) is based mostly on the past, your experiences, as well as your traditions, beliefs and perhaps some nebulous incidents that took place in the past, but of which you were not aware. However, there are times when the program may include negative codes (also called errors in programming language) that could hinder the efficiency of your mind, limiting your ability to achieve.

The purpose of positive affirmation is to eliminate the negative messages or get rid of the bugs, so that you can stay with the perfect program (mindset) that maximizes your capabilities.

With this analogy, it is easy to discover some reasons why you need affirmations that are positive. The reasons listed below are easy to discover:

Eliminate the faulty mindset that blocks your ability to achieve.

Rewrite (re-code) your mental state to allow you to replace the gap caused by thought patterns (bugs) with positive code.

Continue to test your mind by improving and strengthening your positive thinking skills.

Ensure that there is no space (cracks) for negative thoughts (bugs) to enter.

Keep activating your mental state (software) to ensure that it will be reliable to complete your work (bodily actions)

Achieve your highest ambitions Dreams and goals

Helping others to realize their full potential by demonstrating compassion and sharing the benefits of positive thinking

Creative visualization

The process of creative visualization refers to a thought-based procedure by which one creates visual mental images for the purpose of recreating or simulating visual perception in order to explore, enhance and transform those images with the intention of reassigning mental labels, or reprogramming their interpretations to achieve and reap psychological and physiological, emotional or social effects.

In essence, creative visualization (or creative meditation) is a form of meditation that allows you to imagine an ideal state of mind by looking at the good and positive side of your nature. In this way it is possible to eliminate negative images by replacing it with a positive one that allows you to build your mental and physical character by including gratitude for appreciation, patience, humility, empathy, love, gratitude, compassion, joy and happiness.

Is creative visualization really a method used to treat dark psychology as well as white psychology?

As with the other tools mentioned above, creative visualization can serve two purposes, depending on the objective.

Like affirmation and positive thinking, it can also be used by manipulators to prepare Dark manipulative tactics.

Benefits of creative visualization as a tool of White Psychology

The beneficial effects of creative visualization a White psychological tool are:

- Reduction of physical pain

* Healing of wounds in the body

* Remedy psychological traumas such as stress, traumatic depression, anxiety, sadness and low mood.

* Increasing self-confidence and self-esteem.

* Improve coping mechanisms in stressful social interactions.

It is possible to see these as some of the issues that make people more vulnerable to emotional and psychological manipulative behaviors.

Mental imagery, both visual and non-visual

Neuroplasticity (or simply reprogramming your brain) You are able to create various types of mental images that differ from visual images, thus recreating the desired experience of perception that encompasses all senses and modalities.

Some of these sensory modalities are:

* Visualization of smells through olfactory imagery.

* Haptic imagery of touch (e.g., texture pressure, temperature [hot, cold, warm, freezing, etc.)

* Auditory imagery of sounds

* Motor imagery of movement

* Taste images of tastes

Taking a look at these sensory modalities, it is easy to see how imaginative visualization could be effortlessly combined with NLP to produce a powerful hypnosis effect. This same blend can be employed to increase the effectiveness of seduction.

How creative visualization can be performed

The creative visualization process can be linked to guided imagery in the guided imagery component of creative visualization in which an external entity (a teacher) instructs students (the visualizer) to trigger and create certain mental images that recreate or reproduce the sensation of one or more particular sensory modes.

Phases of creative visualization

The main phases of creative visualization are described below:

Phase 1: Generation of the image.

In this phase the mental image is invoked or generated by memories, imagination (fantasy) or both.

Phase 2. Image maintenance

In this phase, deliberate efforts are made to maintain or sustain the generated image. The generated image is usually short-lived if it is not intentionally maintained. Maintenance is crucial to ensure that the imaging process is capable of moving to the next stage, inspection.

Phase 3: Image inspection

In this stage the image is examined for clarity, analyzed for dimensions and finally interpreted. This requires taking the image and scanning it in all its dimensions to determine its possible interpretations by the participant.

Phase 4 Image transformation

At this point, the user alters, modifies or transforms the mental image through the process of remapping or reprogramming, or both. Remapping is the process of recreating the image into a different image that has a particular meaning. Reprogramming is the re-imagining of the meaning of a particular mental image.

From a brief overview of the steps involved in creating creative visualization, you will quickly see why it is very easy to combine the two with NLP and meditation to make an even more powerful tool for seduction and hypnotization.

Chapter 5: Mental Manipulation and Emotional Exploitation

Manipulation is the art of arranging your options on the chessboards of life to enable you to achieve your desired goal. It is about carefully arranging the conditions to work in your favor.

Manipulation techniques of various types

There are many types of manipulation. These are the most commonly used

* Psychological manipulation

* Social manipulation

Social manipulation is group-based. It can involve the manipulation of relationships within a specific group. In the context of social manipulation, we could have manipulation of the political system control of the media and religion military manipulation, etc. The main agent of manipulation of social systems is Social Engineering.

In this chapter we will focus on the manipulation of individuals and we will focus on emotional manipulation and psychological manipulation.

General characteristics of manipulators

Before we dive into the psychological and emotional aspects of manipulation Let's consider "what is the single characteristic that makes someone an effective manipulator?"

The characteristics of manipulators.

They have mastered the art of moving smoothly through obstacles - people, situations.

* They are street smart: they are able to protect themselves,

use the power of authority to their advantage and bypass rules and laws when they are safer, etc.

* They are not afraid to use dark psychology techniques, including deception, persuasion, seduction, brain manipulation, hypnosis, etc. in order to achieve their goals.

They know that experience and skill alone are not enough to distinguish them from the rest of the herd, and the need for survival strategies is a necessity.

* They have mastered the art of disguising their activities to operate in the shadows. They have mastered the art of concealing secret tactics.

Manipulation techniques

* Gaslighting - using counter-narratives to make someone doubt themselves and then take control of the reasoning process. For example, the manipulator may say things, but then act as if they didn't really say them. In the process, you begin to question whether you were listening to the person who said it or whether you were lost in thought. They can disrupt your routine and cause you to become dependent as soon as you lose focus.

* Delegating - applying persuasion tactics, reward tactics and other strategies to allow others to do the work for you. You may do this with the intention of getting your bosses to recognize you as a leader... which can lead to the opportunity for promotion.

* A deliberate misinterpretation

* An iron fist

Warning indicators that you are in the arms of a risky manipulator.

These are the warning signs to watch out for if you suspect you are in the clutches of manipulators

Your words will be used against you

Your vulnerabilities can be exploited to your advantage

* The disguise comes as a form of help only to make you more miserable

* They can make you feel guilty (projection of guilt)

* They make you feel dissatisfied in your relationship, but make you afraid of losing it.

They make you feel like you don't meet their expectations.

* You feel isolated from them

* If you don't accept their demands, they take their affection and love away from you.

* They purposely make a statement that is annoying to irritate you and then claim that you did not understand their words.

Psychological (mental) manipulation

Psychological manipulation is the process of altering a person's mindset (attitudes, beliefs and behaviors) to achieve a specific goal.

From the beginning of the book we have discussed the different types of psychology, focusing on dark psychology as well as white psychology. We have also discussed the different types of manipulation techniques and tools.

In this chapter we are going to examine the main characteristics of psychological manipulators and the signs that tell you that you are being psychologically controlled.

The signs of psychological manipulation

These are typical indicators of the psychological skills of manipulators:

* They are skilled victims who always claim fault and insist that you apologize, even if they were involved in the incident.

* They will always make use of the word "love" as a means to manipulate you "if you really loved me then it would not be a crime to do this".

* They will push you to question your mental sanity and, as a result, make you feel emotionally and mentally confused - they employ gaslighting.

They will always wish to have you in their mental and emotional world, yet make no real effort to connect with yours For example, they tell stories about their problems to gain your sympathy, but show no interest in your own personal predicaments.

* They use the weapon of silence when they are emotionally agitated. When you experience a problem, particularly one for which they are responsible for occurring, they are quiet or cold, so that you resemble the person in your head.

* They make no effort to show responsibility for the emotional wreckage they force on you. For example, they may cause you pain, but never admit to being sorry.

* They always try to discredit your feelings. If you try to convey your emotions, they quickly obscure them by substituting their own thoughts and feelings, making your feelings seem invalid.

*Triangulation is the constant effort to add an extra dimension to an existing relationship between two individuals with the goal of breaking it. In essence, they insert their own emotional angle to those of the other emotional angles...that's why they triangulate. They are similar to a horn that shatters the relationship. Triangulators are common in relationships. It can be a friend who flirts or seduces your girlfriend, or boyfriend before taking them away. They are also present in politics.

* Triangulators explode when they detect a mistake. They scream, shout and shout to drown out their voice.

* Powerful dependents are those who appear weak and appear vulnerable to get help from people who care about their needs.

* Pretends love and compassion.

"Plays the innocence game," feigning total disbelief and confusion when accused of committing a crime.

* Excessive aggressiveness: uses angry outbursts to slap his victims into submission.

* Denial

* Truth is spun

- Frequently fluctuating moods this makes the patient unbalanced.

* Love bombardment, followed by an immediate loss of courage.

How do psychological manipulators carry out their manipulation plan?

The following are some of the most common ways psychological manipulators carry out their strategy:

* Restitution of facts (creating alternative facts).

* Building the field advantage

* First, let him talk to allow him to determine his base, and capitalize on his weaknesses.

* Flooding you with statistics and facts (in essence, forcing you into his mental territory, where you are vulnerable)

* Overwhelm you with bureaucracy (in essence, forcing you into his mental territory, where you are vulnerable)

* Overwhelm you with bureaucracy that is complex and with completely unnecessary procedures

Taking advantage of negative surprises, e.g., waiting until the end of negotiations to announce surprise items that reduce the value of what is about to be concluded.

Make sure you do not impose an excessive time limit on decision making, to avoid ending up making irrational decisions.

Using a negative tone of voice in the hope of destroying your self-confidence and self-esteem.

* Constantly judging you in a negative way to make you feel unworthy.

* Feigning ignorance, especially when knowledge of the facts may be advantageous to them.

* Accusation of guilt: pushing you into situations where they might accuse you, see you in a negative light or force you to apologize. In the end, putting you at a superior psychological advantage.

* Playing victimhood by using exaggeration to gain sympathy or achieve martyrdom. In most cases, will use your feeling of goodwill, responsibility and empathy. and to gain undeserved gain or to get a concession.

* Moving the goalposts

* Not compromising

* Distraction from the discussion to avoid certain issues * Distraction from the discussion to avoid certain issues

* Flattery

* Sarcasm

Typical characteristics of psychological manipulators.

We have looked at the obvious evidence of psychological manipulators and the method they use to carry out their plan.

The question remains: what is the characteristic that helps them succeed in their field?

Listed below are some of the traits inherent in the typical psychological manipulator:

* Idea sower - subtly and passively, he keeps sowing new ideas that basically, are meant to provide him with personal advantages. He offers the concepts, entices you to deal with them and then keeps the benefits for himself.

* Constant inquisitor who makes use of negative probes as a tool of criticism. The main objective is to make you feel inferior and the inquisitor superior.

- Selective listener who sifts through your thoughts and words to gather information with which to influence you.

* Reverse psychologists try to stop you from doing what they want you to do, knowing full well that you are more likely to do it because they are dissuading you. They may also persuade you to perform an action that they do not want you to do, but they know for certain that you will not perform it. Their main goal is to make you feel more secure or strengthen it for their own benefit.

* Constant victimhood - continually plays the victim role

even when in a position of guilt, to ward off any possible consequences of responsibility.

* The masked braggart employs subtle methods to create a feeling of less than. He uses a "know it all" approach, and then routinely tries to correct you, if only by trying to make your equivalents to your words seem more superior, even if they are not in context.

* The projector projects the mental image inside you in a way that overwhelms your personal mental image.

"Deliberate misinterpreter" - - they make up their own interpretations to fit their personal perspective. This can include the use of similes, antonyms and synonyms and proverbs, quotes, etc. to determine the meaning that is different from the statement.

Manipulation of emotions

Indicators that signal that one is in the hands of an emotional manipulator.

* Killing with kindness

* Convenient need

* Exuding a calm, soothing and serene attitude

* Always "having fun

* Using emotional blackmail "I can't do anything in the absence of your help", "I will kill myself if I leave you", "I will die without you", etc.

* Turning to you (field advantage)

* Inspiring your heartstrings (it would be silly for people to do the same), "if you have an ounce of heart, keep me in your thoughts", etc.

* Cheap compliments and flattery

* Excessive generosity

How can I avoid being manipulated?

Here are some general guidelines to help you avoid all forms of manipulative actions:

Don't be afraid to say "no."

Stand your ground

Learn to read what is in your environment:

* body language - stiffness, tension and use of gestures to mislead.

* body posture - forcefulness when posing in order to take control of your body

* eye contact - problems making eye contact. If contact is made, it feels as if it is penetrating. It is uncomfortable in duration and intensity.

* tone of voice - powerful (to be dominant, especially by superiors) and nervous (to lie coyly, especially by subordinates) or altered (in cases of seduction by persuasion, etc.)

Use your intuition to guide you: the sixth sense is able to guide you out of a difficult or unpleasant circumstance. The sixth sense is innate in us humans, as in all animals. It is used above all for survival. It is lost when we do not trust it. It is gained when we trust in the ability.... It can be prone to learn not to use it.

Chapter 6: What to do Victimhood detected victims of dark psychological manipulation.

Victimhood is one of the strongest, most reliable and powerful indicators of manipulation. Therefore, it is vital that you learn the art of identifying victims of dark psychological manipulation. In this way, you will not only assist them but also discern yourself if you perceive that you are falling into the hands of a dark psychology manipulator.

In the next chapter we will examine the signs that help identify victims of dark psychological manipulation.

We will examine some of the victims listed below:

Victims of indoctrination

Victims of brainwashing

Victims of hypnotization

Victims of psychological manipulation

Victims of persecution

How to identify indoctrination victims

Victims of indoctrination exhibit certain behavioral traits. These are some of the characteristic traits of people who were indoctrinated:

Self-awareness is not present: individuals lack self-awareness, so they are unable to recognize the different sources of information needed to trigger reflection. In a sense they are aware that they have been brainwashed. However, there is an intense inertial resistance to their awakening. It is as if they are immersed in a dream and would like to wake up and perform actions such as walking, waving, grasping, etc., but their limbs are still in motion. This inertia can be marked by a powerful sense of ignorance which, in the extreme, can manifest itself through arrogance. Hubris actively seeks to deny and discredit any information that is crucial to bring them out of their indoctrination-driven lethargy.

Critical inquiry is a blight: indoctrinated people cannot afford to engage in critical inquiry. Internally, they are scared of the consequences of revealing the truth and verifying the facts. The reason is the price of change. It is like a person who has walked 50 miles to reach a specific destination only to discover that he has made a mistake. Reverse direction and take the left-hand path. There will be much distress. Lack of critical analysis leads to a false belief that is based on the belief that beliefs are truths or even facts. Thus, many indoctrinated people believe in truth.

* They dislike criticism: Indoctrinated individuals become mentally lazy. They fall into a comfort zone, requiring less effort and less energy. They are unwilling to exert more energy and more effort to get out of this comfortable state. They prefer to go through it, rather than reopen their sails to renew their bodies in radical changes. Any thought that makes them think critically is an attack on their peace. They prefer to expend their physical and emotional energy to fight any external force that tries to pull them out of stagnation.

* Blind obedience: In the absence of the ability to critically inquire, without critical thinking, and lacking in self-awareness, the end result is blind obedience to what keeps people stuffed in their comfort zone of moderation. Sometimes, and most of the time, the comfort zone of mediocrity feels so cozy that not many dare venture into the roaring cold wind beyond it. Indoctrinated people are surrounded by a powerful defense of their beliefs. Any challenge to their beliefs is an attempt to destroy their fortress. The only response that can be expected from them. In this way, objective thinking is not a priority...however, any additional training is accepted as long as they see it as helping them feel more comfortable in that particular area.

* Fiercely fierce defense Indoctrinated individuals violently and fiercely defend the system or institution that teaches them. It may be cultured, cultural or political, national or even professional.

* A rapid emotional seizure: The indoctrinated person shows rapid and uncontrollable bouts of emotion when they feel their beliefs are being challenged. They experience the same as soldiers feel when the enemy attacks their fortress or their master.

How can you identify those who are victims of brainwashing?

Many times the person is educated before they are indoctrinated. The opposite can also happen. Thus, both indoctrination and brainwashing are two strategies that can be symbiotic. They can also be employed simultaneously.

Like brainwashing, indoctrinated people exhibit certain behaviors.

Here are some of the behaviors easily displayed by a brainwashed person:

Absolute loyalty and obedience Brainwashed people remain loyal and obedient to the brainwashers who are responsible for them. They are "yes" people who believe they have a duty to follow every promise and directive of their master brainwasher.

* Codependency: Brainwashed people show a high degree of codependency. They always need individuals to look to their master brainwasher for finding and providing solutions, as well as forming opinions, etc. They have no capacity for independent thinking. They cannot afford to build their minds

to think. Therefore, they show the only mental apathy and death of thinking. Without their leader, no decision can be made and no thinking can be done. take.

* Exit from life in general People who have been brainwashed abandon their private life. The brainwashed individual is not able to live an independent life of his own. This is the reason why you see cult followers abandon their homes, spouses and communities, families, etc. to stay with their brainwashers. The brainwashed have no chance of living an independent life. However, the withdrawal from life is not initiated by the brainwasher, but is facilitated and empowered through the mindwashers. The brainwasher always looks for people with mental or psychic problems. Thus, people who have poor self-esteem, low self-worth or lack of confidence, as well as those who feel they have not been successful in their lives are likely victims of brainwashers. The brainwasher takes advantage of the fact that they are withdrawn from their own lives , creating a space in which they can withdraw - their circle.

* Fanaticism: Most brainwashed people are extremely fanatical. They worship their brainwasher with fervor. They direct all their energies to that pursuit. Their passion for adventure can lead them to confront anyone who dares to challenge their brainwasher's authority. They are willing to fight to the death, sacrificing their own interests to defend the brainwasher's selfish needs.

* Obsessive: Those who have been brainwashed are extremely captivated by their brainwasher. They construct the brainwasher as a suffocation and feel insecure about anyone

attempting to invade the master's realm. They are similar to soldiers protecting the king, or drones guarding the queen bee.

* Self-isolation: A method of physically withdrawing from their lives, brainwashed people withdraw from their families or friends, as well as loved ones. They become less interested in their former job, profession or even trade. They are willing to physically separate themselves from those who do not adhere to their brainwasher's rules. This is the path most terrorists follow.

How to Recognize Hypnotization Victims

Hypnotized patients show some of the most visible signs. This makes it much easier to recognize the victim of hypnotization than those who have been subjected to indoctrination and brainwashing.

Here are the signs that can help you recognize a victim of hypnotization:

Eye fixation is the first suggestion hypnotists offer to the person being hypnotized. Without this, hypnotism is unlikely to work.

Pupil dilation is the result of prolonged periods of eye fixation and fixation, pupil dilation is a result.

Changes in blink reflexes In prolonged blinking, the eye begins to lose its reflexes. Most of the time the blinking rhythm slows down abnormally.

Rapid eye movement - Rapid eye movements are a sign that hypnotic stimulation has advanced to a higher level. Rapid eye movements are typical of dreams. In this case the person has lost perspective of the environment, despite suggestions made by the psychic.

The eyelids move

Smoothing of the facial muscles.

The slowing down of the reflux

The reduction of the swallowing reflexes

Immobility of the body

Absorption inside the body

Attention to the response

How can victims of psychological manipulation be identified?

These are the most obvious signs of victims of manipulative psychological methods:

They are captivated by the plethora of information available.

They are submissive in the face of raised voices and angry outbursts.

They blame themselves and their bad relationships.

Doubt their ability to cope with their circumstances

Are prone to self-evaluation

Follow instructions without hesitation

Lack clarity and are unable to make decisions independently of the manipulator

Do not accept being demeaned

Are resisted or avoided by long-time acquaintances because of relationships

Like to be in a quiet place

How victims of perspecticide can be recognized

Perspectivism is a state that causes one to lose one's own

perception of reality. Instead, one is able to get a picture of the person he or she manipulates. In this scenario, the manipulator is usually the narcissist, who wants to profit from the victim's personal gain.

Due to the loss of vision of real life, the person perceives reality according to the mental image elaborated by the narcissist.

These are some of the indicators that you are suffering from perspectivism

Your thoughts, emotions and perceptions are erased by the narcissist. does the same by altering or destroying your thought pattern. The alteration can take the physical, emotional or even emotional form. For example, a narcissistic person will want to disrupt your daily routines such as work, sleep and leisure They will frighten you and create self-doubt and react to your feelings, thoughts and actions, with aggression. they will not acknowledge your feelings and force you into submission.

Are not connected to family, friends and other loved ones. Isolation is the narcissist's weapon to control. To ensure total control over your thoughts the narcissist makes sure to block you from those who can help form your own point of view. Once you are isolated from the above sources, you are left with only the narcissist to validate your point of view. Through induced self-deprecation that eventually leads to the surrender of your personal perspective.

Self-esteem is diminished: The narcissist slanders your self-esteem by gaslighting and eliminating or suppressing your thoughts, feelings and sentiments. At some point, you become incapable of being your true self. In the absence of the narcissist, it's easy to think of yourself as worthless. The narcissist continues to make you feel this way through emotional blackmail, unwarranted negative criticism or even brutal abuse. You then lose confidence in your own beliefs, thoughts and ideas, as well as your beliefs and abilities. You feel ashamed and unworthy. This causes you to fall into accepting the selfish desires of the self-centered narcissist.

* You are micromanaged. The narcissist controls everything you do. When you sleep, how you sleep, when you get up, when you get up and what you do, how you work, where you work, what time you have to enter the dining room, kitchen bathroom, bedroom, etc. everything is controlled. You must ask explicit permission to access these areas. You may be violently awakened to consciousness in the middle of your sleep. Where you shop, what you buy and the amount you spend on purchases has to be controlled and approved. What you think of yourself has to be confirmed by the narcissist in the form of uninvolved comments and recommendations. This means there is no way to do anything for yourself.

Your identity is defined by the narcissist. There is no sense of self-identity other than that defined by the narcissistic person. The narcissist is able to create various negative thoughts about your appearance, character, manner of speech, posture, etc. In order to ensure that you have lost your sense of self-identity. The narcissist creates the type of person he would like to project onto you. This is accomplished by putting the image he has created of himself inside your mind. The real you is hidden. Instead, you rely on the image of a narcissistic you to define you.

* You are subject to the following rules of relationship: The who, time, date, motive, how and why of your relationships with other people is determined by the Narcissist. The Narcissist can set your meeting schedule based on his own preferences, not yours to ensure that he is in a position to schedule you and monitor your behavior. This is accomplished with a carrot and stick policy. You will be rewarded when you adhere to the rules and severely punished if you do not. Violence, love, kindness and brutality are thrown in randomly so that you feel unbalanced and in a position of not being able to define your relationships with others. You then become a victim of trauma bonding. Through traumatic bonding you experience trauma, but instead of avoiding the person causing you pain, you embrace them and are completely dependent on them. It is a form of Stockholm syndrome.

* You are no longer the person you used to be and you are ashamed of your former "freer" self. This is especially true if the narcissist is aware of your past and makes use of your past mistakes to threaten you.

* You struggle to be yourself and transcend the superficial labels the narcissist has placed on you. You are able to communicate within the confines of the mental map that was created for you by your victimized narcissist.

* You feel a lack of control: It feels as if your entire existence is on autopilot. You are a mere participant who has no influence over the way the vehicle that is the life you live is driven. Your only hope is that everything goes smoothly.

* You feel incredibly uncomfortable without your narcissistic victimhood. You fear and panic about what might happen to you without the narcissist's presence. In your mind, it's anxiety about what the abuser who abused you will react to when he or she returns. You believe that you are not capable of being accountable to him and, as such, you are already at fault leaving aside the other things you might have done that will not be to the victim's liking. Naturally, the narcissist will seem to be unhappy that you are not around him, so that you do not have the feeling of freedom.

* You feel that your life lacks purpose. The loss of self-esteem and the inability to lead an independent lifestyle means that all you have left is to serve your self-centered master. There is no reason of your own... because there is no existence of your own. Your vision has been eliminated.

Chapter 7: Tips to protect yourself from falling victim to the manipulation of dark psychology.

It is always better to protect yourself than to cure yourself. There is a certain depth to dark psychology that you cannot get rid of without help from an outside source. Outside assistance is not always reliable. Therefore, the best method is to protect yourself.

The following are the most important steps you can take to avoid becoming a victim of Dark psychological influences:

* Make use of White psychological techniques to benefit from them.

* Learn how to detect Dark psychological predators.

* Don't become a Dark psychological victim.

* Create an army to defend yourself from Dark psychological predators.

Use the tools of White psychology to your advantage. White psychology techniques to benefit you

We talked about this in chapter 4. We talked about Dark and White psychological tools. They are similar to saws - they are capable of cutting both ways. Although used in the hands of Dark psychology, these tools are also used by White psychologists.

For a quick overview, these are the vital White psychological tools you can employ to safeguard yourself from becoming a victim of Dark psychology:

Mindfulness meditation.

Neuro Linguistic Programming (NLP)

Neuroplasticity

Power posture

Positive affirmations and positive thinking

Creative visualization

How to use mindfulness meditation to protect against dark psychological predators

Mindfulness is the process of becoming self-aware. Those who are not self-aware are easy targets to be devoured by dark psychological predators. Like all predators, there is one that is capable of consuming every other type of animal. Therefore, predators choose their prey based on specific characteristics. These are the characteristics you should watch out for. Insanity is the main characteristic of a Dark psychological prey.

We are aware that dark psychological predators can create psychological traps inside your brain. Being self-aware allows you to detect the lures... regardless of whether they are in the form of thoughts, ideas, etc. Being aware of these traps ensures that you don't become entangled.

Meditation is an effective tool that can be combined with mindfulness. It is all about focus and concentration.

Most of the time, the prey of dark psychology is always unfocused. Their minds wander from one idea to another and try to hold on to every attractive idea. Their minds are frantic and have no commitment to their thoughts.

This wandering mind can fall victim to the lures of mind-altering thoughts. manipulative.

By directing yourself to stay focused and concentrate on the things that matter it is possible to stay away from your fundamental mindset and the traps associated with dark psychology.

How NLP is used to defend against the psychological predators of Darkness.

NLP is certainly a powerful tool. If there is one tool that is capable of being used by Dark psychology predators to wreak havoc and that is NLP. However, the same tool can also be employed to combat these predators by those who are capable of using these tools. NLP is a tool for arming and disarming.

NLP is most crucial in combating the negative self-images that cause low self-esteem.

Low self-esteem can be a strong magnet for dark psychological predators. It is like the powerful smell of meat to them. It arouses their hunger to extreme levels of lust. It excites their jaws with its crunch. Like crocodiles do, they attack their prey mercilessly as it lies on the ground.

You can use NLP to alter the mental maps of your brain so that your mental maps do not point to negative images. Instead, changing the meaning of metatags from negative to positive could cause a counter-negative impact.

How to use neuroplasticity to defend against dark psychological predators.

As we mentioned earlier in Chapter 4 The most crucial aspect that is learning to USE neuroplasticity.

You are able to benefit from how your brain works in order to effectively use resources in order to change in order to avoid things that are not in your best interest.

For example, seduction is the most effective weapon to manipulate emotions. In most cases, dark psychology predators use sexual or gender seduction to lure their prey. Neuroplasticity allows you to alter your brain wiring to match the learned non-utilization of specific sexual signals that are often susceptible to Dark seductive predators.

How to apply power techniques to protect yourself from Dark psychological predators.

One of the main characteristics of Dark psychological prey is low self-confidence. Self-confidence problems stem from low self-esteem that is caused by a self-image that is negative. We have looked at how NLP can help change the meta labels in your mind to drive away a negative self-image. But NLP alone may not reveal that aspect of your external environment that scares away predators.

In nature, we can appreciate how a confident, assertive posture helps scare away potential predators.

A predator is extremely analytical. A predator evaluates

the risks versus the rewards of pouncing on potential prey. Instinctively, if the risk is high enough that the predator is more likely to be crushed than to have the opportunity to eat, it will not take on a risky experience.

Therefore, having confidence and a dominant posture can help you ward off potential psychological predators in the dark.

Power Posing involves using your body posture to express the posture of confidence in yourself.

Some of the most powerful Power poses are:

* Looking at the potential Predator with sharpness and straightness in your eyes. This can help prevent deceptive characters from being detected.

* Appearing confident and emotionless This will make you appear weaker and will ward off seducers.

- Adopting an upright, straight and bold posture this will deter those who are narcissistic and are adept at using intimidation techniques to force their victims to constantly submit and give in.

5How to use positive thoughts along with positive affirmations to protect yourself from the predators of dark psychology

Like meditation and mindfulness, positive thoughts and affirmations are two distinct tools. However, they are most effective when used together.

Positive affirmations and positive thinking reinforce each other in a cyclical fashion to increase strength and power.

But, mindfulness, NLP and neuroplasticity are extremely important tools for fine-tuning positive thinking and positive affirmation. They allow positive affirmations and positive thinking to become reality, rather than the mind talking about it.

Here are some of the ways to use a mixture of positive thinking and affirmation to deal with dark psychological predators:

When a dark predator puts you in an unfavorable situation, the goal is to force you to doubt yourself. Your reaction may be

Positivity: I am aware of what this person wants. I am not who I say I am.

Positive affirmation that I am complete and beautifully created.

How to use creative visualization to protect yourself from dark psychological predators.

In Chapter 4 of the book, creative visualization is the process of creating a mental image that you want to visualize and harnessing your energy to manifest it.

We have also observed that Dark Psychological manipulators plant negative images of themselves in their victims, so that they can force them into low self-esteem, a state that is their own turf.

Creative visualization, like NLP, allows you to stay focused on the ideal self-image and consequently stay away from a negative self-image that does not match the reality of your life.

You can use creative visualization to build your own image of who you would like to be in the coming years. Examples:

* A successful career-oriented wife or husband.

* A successful, freewheeling entrepreneur

* A hard-nosed, independent thinker who is a strong optimist

* etc.

After you create the image, you experience it as if it is already there. It's like creating an outline of your ideal house, and then feeling like you live in it. In reality, you live in the house.... for the moment! It is not your intention to live there in the near future, once you have built it. No! It is possible to remove that disconnect known as "future" from the image. You can make use of the dissociative tool of NLP, to remove the "future" disconnect.

Then, there is some chance that a psychopath or self-centered sadist will appear and tell you "You have no home, you are worthless. You can take what I am providing you (such as my sex object in my house) as a better option than your worthlessness."

Without the image you have built up of a decent, respect-ful, safe place to call your own, you are more likely to fall into self-doubt when you step under the weight of a psychopath with a narcissistic personality.

Creative visualization can help you avoid being a victim Dark psychology .

With the help of imagination you can create a different reality. Not a false one, but one that is real because you are able to direct your attention and focus on gradual realization.

Creative visualization is not just a fantasy. It's about "keep getting there." You live in the image you have made and work to achieve it every second of your life. It's like playing a video online. It's impossible to watch all the scenes at once. At every step, frames appear and you watch it. The frames move in a seamless, continuous pattern, so you don't realize that there are hundreds or even thousands of images flowing through this movie. Are you not able to imagine that you will be able to create more frames as you watch new ones appear? This is exactly what the episodes are about.

Creative visualization is the process of creating your own movie of your life. You experience the moment it comes to life. You experience it as you create more scenes and put the scenes in the frame. There is no waiting. There is no need to be trapped in the waiting that is known as "future." You live in the present episode and continue to wait for the next installment. There is no disconnect between your daily life and the movie. How can you afford to lose focus? Don't.

Be able to spot the dark predators.

Every prey's life depends on the ability to identify its prey. This is the initial and most important step in the survival of the fittest.

Every day that the predator is alive is proof that the prey has lost its life. If you are alive it simply indicates that you have survived long enough to see the predator in its prime. To stay alive, you have to be vigilant.

To recognize a predator, you have to be able to recognize:

A clear picture of the character of your prey.

Clear attributes will help you identify this image.

Make sure you profile your predator correctly.

Beware of becoming an obscure prey

It is normal for there to be prey and predators. However, it is also normal for certain prey species to be able to stay away from falling victim to predators and have a long and satisfying life.

Regardless of the number of dark psychological predators, many of them in disguise, you can avoid being their prey.

Here are some steps you should take to avoid becoming the next victim:

Always be mindful and alert: you will only identify predators when you are aware. The mindfulness practice we have discussed can help in this regard.

Improve your self-defense system Even with the highest level of alertness, it's normal to have moments when you fall asleep... to allow your brain to shut down and recharge your mind. In these moments you can be vulnerable. As with the powerful goring of a buffalo, or the deadly kicks of a giraffe you could provide a predator with a story he won't forget... should you survive. That means you must be equipped with strong protective tools in case you are accidentally caught.

You must be fast and react quickly - The only thing that can prevent an antelope from becoming the next victim of a predator is the ability to be quick, agile and swift in your reaction. In addition, its flight mechanism must be at its maximum. Certain predators are more formidable and cannot behave like a buffalo elephant. It is only possible to flee to avoid being held. If you learn of the possibility of a dictatorship in the army and you are not able to fight for yourself and prevail. The only way to not be a captive of theirs is to flee...to a safe haven elsewhere. In that safe haven you can figure out how to stand up to the dictatorship, muster enough energy and resources to challenge and defy their system of government. It is a strategy of retreat.

Build a Defense Army to defend yourself against dark psychological predators.

The buffalo have perfected the art of defeating the lions. It is due to their cooperation. A lone lion is not capable of taking on a herd of buffalo. He will not only be defeated, but also killed...that is if he is not able to fly successfully.

Unity is a powerful thing. The union of the mind.

It is this union of mind that produces powerful religions. It is this union of mind that causes effective revolution. It is this unity of mind that fends off foreign attacks on a nation.

We are aware of how religious groups spread their message to gain new followers. It usually starts with one person, but a large number of followers and adherents follow. You are never alone when you possess a strong mind. There are many possible minds that are attracted to your thoughts that can coalesce around your brain and be able to become part of your mind. History has proven this, as it will prove it. As long as the human mind remains the same throughout our history, this is possible.

Although revolutions can alter the functioning of the mind, however, they are not capable of altering the nature of the mind. The nature of the mind is altered through a slow and gradual process of evolution and is not within the conscious control of the human mind. Most of our unconscious and subconscious mind is still in the process of investigation. Without this breakthrough could the character of the human mind be changed? This is not likely... but its direction and orientation. This means that by gaining a better understanding of the nature of the human mind and its nature capable of using the same methods and tools employed by religious pundits, political gurus, educational gurus, military experts, and others, to achieve their goals and objectives that is, to build one of the forces of protection against dark psychological predators.

As buffaloes are aware, like other animals that rely on their mental chemistry, that it will always be important to build an elite defense against dark psychology predators... in case they take you for a ride and then eat your body to the extent of their previous dinners.

It is to ensure your own survival that you join this mastermind group against the dark beasts.

Chapter 8: What you can do is to cleanse yourself of the toxins of Dark Psychology.

If you understand how the spider works and how it operates, you will quickly understand the ways in which a dark psychological predator operates.

The spider creates a trap in the form of a web. The web is constructed in such a way that it not only traps its prey, but also alerts it when it has been caught. The web is constructed so that it has an easy route on the Internet to reach the trapped prey.

When the prey has been trapped and the spider has been alerted and flies off to inject the victim with venom. Once the prey is injected, the spider goes back to sleep until the venom is subdued and finally eliminates the prey.

Dark psychology predators function in a similar way.

By understanding the structure of their web and, more importantly, the nature in their venom, it is possible to rid their body of the effects of the venom. Being aware that a spider cannot devour its prey even if it is alive, the only way to get rid of it is to keep injecting it with venom. If the venom does not work and the predator is not able to take it, it is likely to let it go... in case it has gained enough strength to get out of the capture web.

Unlike houseflies, and other similar insects, we possess an enormous amount of cognitive power... provided it is used properly. Therefore, the most important secret is how you use your brain power to defeat potential predators.

Just like any other detoxification agent, it is essential to know what the poison does. By knowing the key component of the poison you will be able to create your detox solution.

We have already looked at some types of poisons (or toxins). These include;
* Dark Persuasion
* Deception
* Deception
* Indoctrination
* Brainwashing
* Dark seduction
* Hypnotization
* Psychological manipulation
However, when it comes to dealing with poisons, it is most effective to detoxify snake venoms, as they are medically complex, since cases of fatal or near-fatal poisoning by snakes

are much more common than those of spiders. There are some spiders whose venom can cause death to humans.

We have also noted the species of animals (also known as snakes) that are venomous:

* Narcissists

* Machiavellians

* Psychopaths

There are many subspecies within each.

Being able to determine the species of a snake makes it simple to determine the type of venom it is capable of using in the event of a bite and an emergency response. In addition, being able to determine the type of dark psychological predator can help determine the type of detoxification you should seek in the event of an attack.

In general, however, you need to be equipped with all possible detox substances, as you cannot know which one will attack you.

How you can detox from dark psychological effects

1- Basic ingredients for your powerful detoxification

Whatever detox you create, the following are the basic ingredients to include in your formulation:

Develop a positive mindset and eliminate the negative mindset.

Create a positive mental image of yourself and eliminate negative self-images

Adopt non-limiting beliefs and erase limiting beliefs

Develop positive habits and let go of bad habits

Achieve a high level of emotional intelligence

Develop critical thinking skills

Engage in the ongoing routine of researching and critically examining yourself

Can challenge your comfort zone by embracing change and being unique

Try different ways of being

With these ingredients, you can add additional ingredients to create customized ingredients to help you cleanse yourself of specific types of poisons.

Chapter 9: Can dark psychology have a silver lining?

In our summary we have examined the example of a weapon as an instrument. It is a weapon that can be used to defend and to attack.

A thief or a serial killer might employ a weapon to carry out evil motives. A weapon can be used with the intention of safeguarding your life or the lives of your loved ones from murderers and robbers.

Although the act of murder is a loss of life, the likelihood of being convicted or not will depend on the intent behind the killing. For example, killing as a result of an accident that is not caused by any fault or carelessness on your part will not be considered a crime that can result in a conviction. In self-defense, killing someone because you took proportionate action against the threat will not result in a conviction.

If the person you killed had a significant share of fault, such as provocation, it is considered manslaughter, since you were provoked, but could have controlled yourself. If this were not the case, and without the victim being provoked to act, you would not have to resort to manslaughter because you were not premeditating the act. On the other hand, killing an innocent person with premeditation is murder. In the case of murder, you will receive the maximum punishment possible under the law, which is life imprisonment or the death penalty.

Therefore, the most important factor is not the act itself, but the intention that drives the act. In the case of criminals, it is the motive rather than the form that counts. A similar distinction can be drawn between white psychology and dark psychology. In reality, it is not the techniques or tools used, but the intention behind the application that makes the major distinction between white and dark psychology.

So, can dark psychological research have an optimistic effect? Yes, it certainly can. The upside of dark psychology is that it can be used to achieve good purposes, even though it may seem ugly.

Yes, counterinsurgency, counterterrorism and counter-intelligence personnel employ Dark techniques to penetrate the enemy, obtain information and deter criminals who pose a danger. If they do not employ dark psychology techniques they will not be successful in defending the public from the threats of these criminal organizations.

In civil cases, the tools and techniques of Dark psychology are used in setting up, obtaining evidence and arresting the corrupt. For example, counterfeit and chemically treated coins are used against corrupt public officials who demand payments in the form of bribes.

When dealing with drug traffickers, police officers employ techniques of deception as well as mental manipulation to appear to be potential customers and, in turn, catch drug traffickers.

As you can see, the same dark psychology tactics are employed, albeit with good intentions.

In the same way, dark psychology techniques and techniques can be used to deal with psychopaths who are dangerous such as serial killers and serial rapists. There are numerous cases where these groups have been crushed through the use of hypnotism and mental manipulation and dark seduction, deception and other methods, thus protecting potential victims from danger.

Take the example of kidnappers who demand a ransom to free their captives and, if they do not get it, kill them. All possible means have been employed to rescue captives. One of the most commonly used methods is deception, in which the ransom is carefully set up as an inducement for them to accept it. Sometimes mental manipulation is used, when the ransom is too high and will not be accepted. Deception, hypnotism or even seduction may be used to divert their attention, and then snipers are strategically placed to eliminate their efforts.

Fortunately, we possess the inherent possibility of utilizing the psychology of darkness. The potential is hidden in our subconscious mind. All we have to do is bring it to light and then consciously guide it toward good intentions, whatever form they take.

We have talked before about the techniques and tools used in dark psychology. It is important to distinguish them from bad intentions and use them to achieve positive purposes.

Chapter 10: How to make use of the positive power of dark psychology to achieve your best goals.

In Chapter 9 we looked at how dark psychology has been used to benefit people. We saw how dark psychology was successfully used in the following cases:

Counterterrorism

Counterinsurgency

Counter-hostage

Anti-corruption

Fight against drug trafficking

Fight against rape

and against serial killers.

There are cases where the flame is used to stop it. It is a common practice employed by farmers... for example, to light small fires and spread them over a strip of land to prevent the larger flame from spreading to the opposite part of the land.

In the medical field, vaccines are used to combat a variety of bacteria and viruses. Vaccines are composed of live bacteria that can be introduced into the human body to serve as a shield against foreign bacteria.

So how do you learn from these cases? What can you do to harness the potential that dark psychology has to achieve what you desire? This is not a call to encourage you to use Dark psychology to carry out the evil motives of others, but rather to make use of Dark psychology to help you achieve good goals that enhance your well-being as well as enhance the greater good of others.

In the fight against terrorists

Terrorism is a common occurrence today. It is impossible

to imagine that you are somehow protected from it. There are cases where anti-terrorism resources are not available or not available until too late. If you happen to be the victim. Terrorists are looking for certain types of people to assassinate.

The most important thing you will need at this point is deception. You must quickly figure out their target and quickly pretend that you are the victim. For example, if there is an attacker who wants to kill people who belong to a certain religious perspective, what should you do? You should quickly assert that you are not a member of that particular religion and do your best to practice that person's religion. That means you have to be attentive to the events around you, and also learn a few things about different religions.

There are people who have saved themselves from being hit by a bullet just by learning something about a different religion or language, another culture, etc. So, don't pass up the opportunity to learn something new.

As opposed to the sex of

There are areas where the prevalence of rape is high. If you find yourself within one of those areas it is essential to master some dark psychology techniques. There are some who have avoided rape by using hypnosis. Some have avoided rape by using reverse psychology. Some have been able to avoid rape by applying dark persuasion.

Being able to quickly recognize weaknesses in the rapist's mind is a great advantage. This is because a strategy applicable to one individual may not be the same for another, as he may not have the same motivation to commit rape.

Facing kidnappers

Many stories have been told of people who have managed to get out of hostage takers' prisons unharmed.

The most effective dark psychology techniques against hostage takers comprise:

* Dark persuasion

* Deception

* Dark seduction

* Dark psychological manipulation

* Reverse psychology

* Hypnotization

These are the typical objectives of the use of these instruments:

* Attenuate the mind of the abductors to allow them to leave. For example, this can be done by using hypnotic induction.

Reverse psychology can make them see the logic of letting you go. For example, "I'm in the same boat as you, so don't punish me by keeping me in a cage."

* Take advantage of the innocent nature of their instincts. For example, you can paternalize (in the case of a male hostage) or maternalize (in the case of a female hostage) the hostage taker. For example, use appealing phrases that draw attention to the instinct, such as "my beautiful son." This is especially useful in the case of a kidnapper who is an alcoholic or psychopath.

Confronting corrupt public officials

In those jurisdictions prone to corruption, where public officials demand payment of a bribe to offer their services and there is an effective anti-corruption agency, it is possible to employ trickery and deception as a way of catching corrupt officials.

For example, you could get document processing from an anti-corruption organization that can be used to prove your case or wear body cameras to document your plan to bribe the official. Pen cameras or button cameras attached to your glasses can be very discreet.

Against drug dealers

Drug addiction is one of the most serious threats to our society today. In our current age, it is difficult to find a community where certain young people are not devastated by this scourge and have become zombies incapable of pursuing any meaningful goal to improve their health and the well-being of the entire community.

Therefore, participating in stopping this drug plague is a huge benefit, not only to you, but to your family members, friends, neighbors and everyone else. You never know, your brother, your daughter, your son or even a friend could be their next victim.

Therefore, it is crucial to understand how to use the power techniques of dark psychology to make an impact on society.

Just as in the fight against corruption, you could set traps for drug dealers. For example, you could appear as a representative of a potential client. With the support of law enforcement or a secret camera, as well as deal notes, you may be able to catch them. Deception can be used to bring them into your "court," where they will not be able to extort money from you.

Mastery of deception or dark persuasion, as well as mind

manipulation, can dramatically increase your ability to recognize the threat and bring it to an end, at least within your own vicinity.

CONCLUSION

I wish that this book has helped you master the techniques of dark psychology and discover the hidden manipulation techniques that will not only enable you to combat those who are using these tricks against your success, but also to apply them to create your own great success.

In addition, I hope it has motivated you enough to share the details of this book with your friends and loved ones so that they too will be able to understand the mysteries of dark psychology that affect our behavior and the most effective techniques of manipulation and methods of persuasion so that they too will have the opportunity to make the most of their lives.